IN MEMORY OF
BROOKE UMBEL
GIVEN BY
HER GRANDMOTHER AND GRANDFATHER
BETTY AND DICK UMBEL

Modern Critical Interpretations

Franz Kafka's
The Metamorphosis

Modern Critical Interpretations

These and other titles in preparation

Modern Critical Interpretations

Franz Kafka's
The Metamorphosis

Edited and with an introduction by
Harold Bloom
Sterling Professor of the Humanities
Yale University

Chelsea House Publishers
NEW YORK ◊ PHILADELPHIA

Library of Congress Cataloging-in-Publication Data
Franz Kafka's The metamorphosis / edited and with an introduction by
Harold Bloom.
     p. cm. — (Modern critical interpretations)
     "A representative selection of the best critical interpretations of
Kafka's crucial narrative. The metamorphosis" — P.
     Bibliography: p.
     Includes index.
     Contents: Gregor Samsa and modern spirituality / Martin
Greenberg — Metamorphosis of the metaphor / Stanley Corngold — The
dramatic in Kafka's Metamorphosis / Evelyn Torton Beck — The
metamorphosis / Ronald Gray — The metamorphosis, Freud, and the
chains of Odysseus / David Eggenschwiler — The impersonal narrator of
The metamorphosis / Roy Pascal — From Marx to myth: the structure
and function of self-alienation in Kafka's Metamorphosis / Walter H.
Sokel — Kafka and Sacher-Masoch / Mark M. Anderson.
     ISBN: 1-55546-070-4
     1. Kafka, Franz, 1883–1924. Verwandlung. [1. Kafka, Franz,
1883–1924. Metamorphosis. 2. German literature — History and
criticism.] I. Bloom, Harold. II. Series.
PT2621.A26V428   1988
833'.912 — dc19   87-17827

Contents

Editor's Note

This book gathers together a representative selection of the best critical interpretations of Kafka's crucial narrative, *The Metamorphosis*, universally regarded as one of the central stories of our spiritual and literary age. The critical essays are reprinted here in the chronological order of their original publication. I am grateful to Hillary Kelleher and Paul Barickman for their assistance in editing this volume.

My introduction sets *The Metamorphosis* in the context of Kafka's unique, unsought position as *the* post-normative Jewish writer, whose work of negation takes place in that rupture between covenanted past and unattainable messianic future. Martin Greenberg begins the chronological sequence of criticism with a close reading that establishes Gregor's transformation as being spiritual, from a death-in-life to a kind of life-in-death.

The process by which metaphor is literalized is seen by Stanley Corngold as the true subject of Kafka's story. In Evelyn Torton Beck's account, we are given a clear sense of the parallels between *The Metamorphosis* and the play, Gordins's *The Savage One*, that Kafka had admired in his passionate investigation of Yiddish theatre.

Comparing *The Metamorphosis* to *In the Penal Colony*, Ronald Gray emphasizes the greater formal control Kafka attains in Gregor Samsa's story, while David Eggenschwiler finds in Gregor's evasive narrative the emergence of the Kafkan avoidance of fixed interpretation that itself becomes the reader's parabolic quest.

Roy Pascal questions the narrator's independence of Gregor, after which Walter Sokel contrasts Kafkan and Marxist myths of alienation. In this book's final essay, Mark M. Anderson reads *The Metamorphosis* alongside Leopold von Sacher-Masoch's *Venus in Furs*, from which Kafka swerves both by starting with Gregor's enslavement, and by a transference of Gregor's bondage from the sexual to the Oedipal realm.

Introduction

In her obituary for her lover, Franz Kafka, Milena Jesenská sketched a modern Gnostic, a writer whose vision was of the *kenoma*, the cosmic emptiness into which we have been thrown:

> He was a hermit, a man of insight who was frightened by life. . . . He saw the world as being full of invisible demons which assail and destroy defenseless man. . . . All his works describe the terror of mysterious misconceptions and guiltless guilt in human beings.

Milena — brilliant, fearless, and loving — may have subtly distorted Kafka's beautifully evasive slidings between normative Jewish and Jewish Gnostic stances. Max Brod, responding to Kafka's now-famous remark — "We are nihilistic thoughts that came into God's head" — explained to his friend the Gnostic notion that the Demiurge had made this world both sinful and evil. "No," Kafka replied, "I believe we are not such a radical relapse of God's, only one of His bad moods. He had a bad day." Playing straight man, the faithful Brod asked if this meant there was hope outside our cosmos. Kafka smiled, and charmingly said: "Plenty of hope — for God — no end of hope — only not for us."

Kafka, despite Gershom Scholem's authoritative attempts to claim him for Jewish Gnosticism, is both more and less than a Gnostic, as we might expect. Yahweh can be saved, and the divine degradation that is fundamental to Gnosticism is not an element in Kafka's world. But we were fashioned out of the clay during one of Yahweh's bad moods; perhaps there was divine dyspepsia, or sultry weather in the garden that Yahweh had planted in the East. Yahweh is hope, and we are hopeless. We are the jackdaws or crows, the kafkas (since that is what the name means, in Czech) whose impossibility is what the heavens signify: "The crows maintain that a single crow could

1

destroy the heavens. Doubtless that is so, but it proves nothing against the heavens, for the heavens signify simply: the impossibility of crows."

In Gnosticism, there is an alien, wholly transcendent God, and the adept, after considerable difficulties, can find the way back to presence and fullness. Gnosticism therefore is a religion of salvation, though the most negative of all such saving visions. Kafkan spirituality offers no hope of salvation, and so is not Gnostic. But Milena Jesenská certainly was right to emphasize the Kafkan terror that is akin to Gnosticism's dread of the *kenoma*, which is the world governed by the Archons. Kafka takes the impossible step beyond Gnosticism, by denying that there is hope for us anywhere at all.

In the aphorisms that Brod rather misleadingly entitled "Reflections on Sin, Pain, Hope and The True Way," Kafka wrote: "What is laid upon us is to accomplish the negative; the positive is already given." How much Kabbalah Kafka knew is not clear. Since he wrote a new Kabbalah, the question of Jewish Gnostic sources can be set aside. Indeed, by what seems a charming oddity (but I would call it yet another instance of Blake's insistence that forms of worship are chosen from poetic tales), our understanding of Kabbalah is Kafkan anyway, since Kafka profoundly influenced Gershom Scholem, and no one will be able to get beyond Scholem's creative or strong misreading of Kabbalah for decades to come. I repeat this point to emphasize its shock value: we read Kabbalah, via Scholem, from a Kafkan perspective, even as we read human personality and its mimetic possibilities by way of Shakespeare's perspectives, since essentially Freud mediates Shakespeare for us, yet relies upon him nevertheless. A Kafkan facticity or contingency now governs our awareness of whatever in Jewish cultural tradition is other than normative.

In his diaries for 1922, Kafka meditated, on January 16, upon "something very like a breakdown," in which it was "impossible to sleep, impossible to stay awake, impossible to endure life, or, more exactly, the course of life." The vessels were breaking for him as his demoniac, writerly inner world and the outer life "split apart, and they do split apart, or at least clash in a fearful manner." Late in the evening, K. arrives at the village, which is deep in snow. The Castle is in front of him, but even the hill upon which it stands is veiled in mist and darkness, and there is not a single light visible to show that the Castle was there. K. stands a long time on a wooden bridge that leads from the main road to the village, while gazing, not at the village, but "into the illusory emptiness above him," where the Castle should be. He does not know what he will always refuse to learn, which is that the emptiness is "illusory" in every possible sense, since he does gaze at the *kenoma*, which resulted initially from the breaking of the vessels, the splitting apart of every world, inner and outer.

Writing the vision of K., Kafka counts the costs of his confirmation, in a passage prophetic of Scholem, but with a difference that Scholem sought to negate by combining Zionism and Kabbalah for himself. Kafka knew better, perhaps only for himself, but perhaps for others as well:

> Second: This pursuit, originating in the midst of men, carries one in a direction away from them. The solitude that for the most part has been forced on me, in part voluntarily sought by me — but what was this if not compulsion too? — is now losing all its ambiguity and approaches its denouement. Where is it leading? The strongest likelihood is that it may lead to madness; there is nothing more to say, the pursuit goes right through me and rends me asunder. Or I can — can I? — manage to keep my feet somewhat and be carried along in the wild pursuit. Where, then, shall I be brought? "Pursuit," indeed, is only a metaphor. I can also say, "assault on the last earthly frontier," an assault, moreover, launched from below, from mankind, and since this too is a metaphor, I can replace it by the metaphor of an assault from above, aimed at me from above.
>
> All such writing is an assault on the frontiers; if Zionism had not intervened, it might easily have developed into a new secret doctrine, a Kabbalah. There are intimations of this. Though of course it would require genius of an unimaginable kind to strike root again in the old centuries, or create the old centuries anew and not spend itself withal, but only then begin to flower forth.

Consider Kafka's three metaphors, which he so knowingly substitutes for one another. The pursuit is of ideas, in that mode of introspection which is Kafka's writing. Yet this metaphor of pursuit is also a piercing "right through me" and a breaking apart of the self. For "pursuit," Kafka then substitutes mankind's assault, from below, on the last earthly frontier. What is that frontier? It must lie between us and the heavens. Kafka, the crow or jackdaw, by writing, transgresses the frontier and implicitly maintains that he could destroy the heavens. By another substitution, the metaphor changes to "an assault from above, aimed at me from above," the aim simply being the signifying function of the heavens, which is to mean the impossibility of Kafkas or crows. The heavens assault Kafka *through his writing*; "all such writing is an assault on the frontiers," and these must now be Kafka's own frontiers. One thinks of Freud's most complex "frontier concept," more complex even than the drive: the bodily ego. The heavens assault Kafka's bodily ego, *but only through his own writing*. Certainly such an assault is not un-Jewish, and has as much to do with normative as with esoteric Jewish tradition.

Yet, according to Kafka, his own writing, were it not for the intervention of Zionism, might easily have developed into a new Kabbalah. How are we to understand that curious statement about Zionism as the blocking agent that prevents Franz Kafka from becoming another Isaac Luria? Kafka darkly and immodestly writes: "There are intimations of this." Our teacher Gershom Scholem governs our interpretation here, of necessity. Those intimations belong to Kafka alone, or perhaps to a select few in his immediate circle. They cannot be conveyed to Jewry, even to its elite, because Zionism has taken the place of messianic Kabbalah, including presumably the heretical Kabbalah of Nathan of Gaza, prophet of Sabbatai Zvi and of all his followers down to the blasphemous Jacob Frank. Kafka's influence upon Scholem is decisive here, for Kafka already has arrived at Scholem's central thesis of the link between the Kabbalah of Isaac Luria, the messianism of the Sabbatarians and Frankists, and the political Zionism that gave rebirth to Israel.

Kafka goes on, most remarkably, to disown the idea that he possesses "genius of an unimaginable kind," one that either would strike root again in archaic Judaism, presumably of the esoteric sort, or more astonishingly "create the old centuries anew," which Scholem insisted Kafka had done. But can we speak, as Scholem tried to speak, of the Kabbalah of Franz Kafka? Is there a new secret doctrine in the superb stories and the extraordinary parables and paradoxes, or did not Kafka spend his genius in the act of new creation of the old Jewish centuries? Kafka certainly would have judged himself harshly as one spent withal, rather than as a writer who "only then began to flower forth."

Kafka died only two and a half years after this meditative moment, died, alas, just before his forty-first birthday. Yet as the propounder of a new Kabbalah, he had gone very probably as far as he (or anyone else) could go. No Kabbalah, be it that of Moses de Leon, Isaac Luria, Moses Cordovero, Nathan of Gaza or Gershom Scholem, is exactly easy to interpret, but Kafka's secret doctrine, if it exists at all, is designedly uninterpretable. My working principle in reading Kafka is to observe that he did everything possible to evade interpretation, which only means that what most needs and demands interpretation in Kafka's writing is its perversely deliberate evasion of interpretation. Erich Heller's formula for getting at this evasion is: "Ambiguity has never been considered an elemental force; it is precisely this in the stories of Franz Kafka." Perhaps, but evasiveness is not the same literary quality as ambiguity.

Evasiveness is purposive; it writes between the lines, to borrow a fine trope from Leo Strauss. What does it mean when a quester for a new Negative, or perhaps rather a revisionist of an old Negative, resorts to the evasion of every possible interpretation as his central topic or theme? Kafka does not doubt guilt, but wishes to make it "possible for men to enjoy sin without guilt, almost without guilt," by reading Kafka. To enjoy sin almost without guilt is to evade interpretation, in exactly the dominant Jewish sense of interpretation. Jewish tradition, whether normative or esoteric, never teaches you to ask Nietzsche's question: "Who is the interpreter, and what power does he seek to gain over the text?" Instead, Jewish tradition asks: "Is the interpreter in the line of those who seek to build a hedge about the Torah in every age?" Kafka's power of evasiveness is not a power over his own text, and it does build a hedge about the Torah in our age. Yet no one before Kafka built up that hedge wholly out of evasiveness, not even Maimonides or Judah Halevi or even Spinoza. Subtlest and most evasive of all writers, Kafka remains the severest and most harassing of the belated sages of what will yet become the Jewish cultural tradition of the future.

II

The jackdaw or crow or Kafka is also the weird figure of the great hunter Gracchus (whose Latin name also means a crow), who is not alive but dead, yet who floats, like one living, on his death-bark forever. When the fussy Burgomaster of Riva knits his brow, asking: "And you have no part in the other world (*das Jenseits*)?", the Hunter replies, with grand defensive irony:

> I am forever on the great stair that leads up to it. On that infinitely wide and spacious stair I clamber about, sometimes up, sometimes down, sometimes on the right, sometimes on the left, always in motion. The Hunter has been turned into a butterfly. Do not laugh.

Like the Burgomaster, we do not laugh. Being a single crow, Gracchus would be enough to destroy the heavens, but he will never get there. Instead, the heavens signify his impossibility, the absence of crows or hunters, and so he has been turned into another butterfly, which is all we can be, from the perspective of the heavens. And we bear no blame for that:

> "I had been glad to live and I was glad to die. Before I stepped aboard, I joyfully flung away my wretched load of ammunition, my knapsack, my hunting rifle that I had always been proud to

carry, and I slipped into my winding sheet like a girl into her marriage dress. I lay and waited. Then came the mishap."

"A terrible fate," said the Burgomaster, raising his hand defensively. "And you bear no blame for it?"

"None," said the hunter. "I was a hunter; was there any sin in that? I followed my calling as a hunter in the Black Forest, where there were still wolves in those days. I lay in ambush, shot, hit my mark, flayed the skin from my victims: was there any sin in that? My labors were blessed. 'The Great Hunter of Black Forest' was the name I was given. Was there any sin in that?"

"I am not called upon to decide that," said the Burgomaster, "but to me also there seems to be no sin in such things. But then, whose is the guilt?"

"The boatman's," said the Hunter. "Nobody will read what I say here, no one will come to help me; even if all the people were commanded to help me, every door and window would remain shut, everybody would take to bed and draw the bedclothes over his head, the whole earth would become an inn for the night. And there is sense in that, for nobody knows of me, and if anyone knew he would not know where I could be found, and if he knew where I could be found, he would not know how to deal with me, he would not know how to help me. The thought of helping me is an illness that has to be cured by taking to one's bed."

How admirable Gracchus is, even when compared to the Homeric heroes! They know, or think they know, that to be alive, however miserable, is preferable to being the foremost among the dead. But Gracchus wished only to be himself, happy to be a hunter when alive, joyful to be a corpse when dead: "I slipped into my winding sheet like a girl into her marriage dress." So long as everything happened in good order, Gracchus was more than content. The guilt must be the boatman's, and may not exceed mere incompetence. Being dead and yet still articulate, Gracchus is beyond help: "The thought of helping me is an illness that has to be cured by taking to one's bed."

When he gives the striking trope of the whole earth closing down like an inn for the night, with the bedclothes drawn over everybody's head, Gracchus renders the judgment: "And there is sense in that." There is sense in that only because in Kafka's world as in Freud's, or in Scholem's, or in any world deeply informed by Jewish memory, there is necessarily sense in everything, total sense, even though Kafka refuses to aid you in getting at or close to it.

But what kind of a world is that, where there is sense in everything, where everything seems to demand interpretation? There can be sense in everything, as J. H. Van den Berg once wrote against Freud's theory of repression, only if everything is already in the past and there never again can be anything wholly new. That is certainly the world of the great normative rabbis of the second century of the Common Era, and consequently it has been the world of most Jews ever since. Torah has been given, Talmud has risen to complement and interpret it, other interpretations in the chain of tradition are freshly forged in each generation, but the limits of Creation and of Revelation are fixed in Jewish memory. There is sense in everything because all sense is present already in the Hebrew Bible, which by definition must be totally intelligible, even if its fullest intelligibility will not shine forth until the Messiah comes.

Gracchus, hunter and jackdaw, is Kafka, pursuer of ideas and jackdaw, and the endless, hopeless voyage of Gracchus is Kafka's passage, only partly through a language not his own, and largely through a life not much his own. Kafka was studying Hebrew intensively while he wrote "The Hunter Gracchus," early in 1917, and I think we may call the voyages of the dead but never-buried Gracchus a trope for Kafka's belated study of his ancestral language. He was still studying Hebrew in the spring of 1923, with his tuberculosis well advanced, and down to nearly the end he longed for Zion, dreaming of recovering his health and firmly grounding his identity by journeying to Palestine. Like Gracchus, he experienced life-in-death, though unlike Gracchus he achieved the release of total death.

"The Hunter Gracchus" as a story or extended parable is not the narrative of a Wandering Jew or Flying Dutchman, because Kafka's trope for his writing activity is not so much a wandering or even a wavering, but rather a repetition, labyrinthine and burrow-building. His writing repeats, not itself, but a Jewish esoteric interpretation of Torah that Kafka himself scarcely knows, or even needs to know. What this interpretation tells Kafka is that there is no written Torah but only an oral one. However, Kafka has no one to tell him what this Oral Torah is. He substitutes his own writing therefore for the Oral Torah not made available to him. He is precisely in the stance of the Hunter Gracchus, who concludes by saying, " 'I am here, more than that I do not know, further than that I cannot go. My ship has no rudder, and it is driven by the wind that blows in the undermost regions of death.' "

III

"What is the Talmud if not a message from the distance?", Kafka wrote to Robert Klopstock, on December 19, 1923. What was all of Jewish tradition, to Kafka, except a message from an endless distance? That is surely part of the burden of the famous parable, "An Imperial Message," which concludes with you, the reader, sitting at your window when evening falls and dreaming to yourself the parable—that God, in his act of dying, has sent you an individual message. Heinz Politzer read this as a Nietzschean parable, and so fell into the trap set by the Kafkan evasiveness:

> Describing the fate of the parable in a time depleted of metaphysical truths, the imperial message has turned into the subjective fantasy of a dreamer who sits at a window with a view on a darkening world. The only real information imported by this story is the news of the Emperor's death. This news Kafka took over from Nietzsche.

No, for even though you dream the parable, the parable conveys truth. The Talmud does exist; it really is an Imperial message from the distance. The distance is too great; it cannot reach you; there is hope, but not for you. Nor is it so clear that God is dead. He is always dying, yet always whispers a message into the angel's ear. It is said to you that: "Nobody could fight his way through here even with a message from a dead man," but the Emperor actually does not die in the text of the parable.

Distance is part of Kafka's crucial notion of the Negative, which is not a Hegelian nor a Heideggerian Negative, but is very close to Freud's Negation and also to the Negative imaging carried out by Scholem's Kabbalists. But I want to postpone Kafka's Jewish version of the Negative until later. "The Hunter Gracchus" is an extraordinary text, but it is not wholly characteristic of Kafka at his strongest, at his uncanniest or most sublime.

When he is most himself, Kafka gives us a continuous inventiveness and originality that rivals Dante, and truly challenges Proust and Joyce as that of the dominant Western author of our century, setting Freud aside, since Freud ostensibly is science and not narrative or mythmaking, though if you believe that, then you can be persuaded of anything. Kafka's beast fables are rightly celebrated, but his most remarkable fabulistic being is neither animal nor human, but is little Odradek, in the curious sketch, less than a page and a half long, "The Cares of a Family Man," where the title might have been translated: "The Sorrows of a Paterfamilias." The family man narrates these five paragraphs, each a dialectical lyric in itself, beginning with one that worries the meaning of the name:

> Some say the word Odradek is of Slavonic origin, and try to account for it on that basis. Others again believe it to be of German

origin, only influenced by Slavonic. The uncertainty of both interpretations allows one to assume with justice that neither is accurate, especially as neither of them provides an intelligent meaning of the word.

This evasiveness was overcome by the scholar Wilhelm Emrich, who traced the name Odradek to the Czech word *odraditi*, meaning to dissuade anyone from doing anything. Like Edward Gorey's Doubtful Guest, Odradek is uninvited yet will not leave, since implicitly he dissuades you from doing anything about his presence, or rather something about his very uncanniness advises you to let him alone:

> No one, of course, would occupy himself with such studies if there were not a creature called Odradek. At first glance it looks like a flat star-shaped spool for thread, and indeed it does seem to have thread wound upon it; to be sure, they are only old, broken-off bits of thread, knotted and tangled together, of the most varied sorts and colors. But it is not only a spool, for a small wooden crossbar sticks out of the middle of the star, and another small rod is joined to that at a right angle. By means of this latter rod on one side and one of the points of the star on the other, the whole thing can stand upright as if on two legs.

Is Odradek a "thing," as the bemused family man begins by calling him, or is he not a childlike creature, a daemon at home in the world of children? Odradek clearly was made by an inventive and humorous child, rather in the spirit of the making of Adam out of the moistened red clay by the J writer's Yahweh. It is difficult not to read Odradek's creation as a deliberate parody when we are told that "the whole thing can stand upright as if on two legs," and again when the suggestion is ventured that Odradek, like Adam, "once had some sort of intelligible shape and is now only a broken-down remnant." If Odradek is fallen, he is still quite jaunty, and cannot be closely scrutinized, since he "is extraordinarily nimble and can never be laid hold of," like the story in which he appears. Odradek not only advises you not to do anything about him, but in some clear sense he is yet another figure by means of whom Kafka advises you against interpreting Kafka.

One of the loveliest moments in all of Kafka comes when you, the paterfamilias, encounter Odradek leaning directly beneath you against the banisters. Being inclined to speak to him, as you would to a child, you receive a surprise: " 'Well, what's your name?' you ask him. 'Odradek,' he says. 'And where do you live?' 'No fixed abode,' he says and laughs; but it is only the kind of laughter that has no lungs behind it. It sounds rather like the rustling of fallen leaves."

"The 'I' is another," Rimbaud once wrote, adding: "So much the worse for the wood that finds it is a violin." So much the worse for the wood that finds it is Odradek. He laughs at being a vagrant, if only by the bourgeois definition of having "no fixed abode," but the laughter, not being human, is uncanny. And so he provokes the family man to an uncanny reflection, which may be a Kafkan parody of Freud's death drive beyond the pleasure principle:

> I ask myself, to no purpose, what is likely to happen to him? Can he possibly die? Anything that dies has had some kind of aim in life, some kind of activity, which has worn out; but that does not apply to Odradek. Am I to suppose, then, that he will always be rolling down the stairs, with ends of thread trailing after him, right before the feet of my children? He does no harm to anyone that I can see, but the idea that he is likely to survive me I find almost painful.

The aim of life, Freud says, is death, is the return of the organic to the inorganic, supposedly our earlier state of being. Our activity wears out, and so we die because, in an uncanny sense, we wish to die. But Odradek, harmless and charming, is a child's creation, aimless, and so not subject to the death drive. Odradek is immortal, being daemonic, and he represents also a Freudian return of the repressed, of something repressed in the *paterfamilias*, something from which the family man is in perpetual flight. Little Odradek is precisely what Freud calls a cognitive return of the repressed, while (even as) a complete affective repression is maintained. The family man introjects Odradek intellectually, but totally projects him affectively. Odradek, I now suggest, is best understood as Kafka's synecdoche for *Verneinung*; Kafka's version (not altogether un-Freudian) of Jewish Negation, a version I hope to adumbrate in what follows.

IV

Why does Kafka have so unique a spiritual authority? Perhaps the question should be rephrased. What kind of spiritual authority does Kafka have for us or why are we moved or compelled to read him as one who has such authority? Why invoke the question of authority at all? Literary authority, however we define it, has no necessary relation to spiritual authority, and to speak of a spiritual authority in Jewish writing anyway always has been to speak rather dubiously. Authority is not a Jewish concept but a Roman one, and so makes perfect contemporary sense in the context of the Roman Catholic Church, but little sense in Jewish matters, despite the squalors of Israeli politics and the flaccid pieties of American Jewish nostalgias. There is no authority without hierarchy, and hierarchy is not a very Jewish concept either. We do not want the rabbis, or anyone else, to tell us what or who is or is not Jewish. The masks of the normative conceal not only the eclecticism of Judaism and of Jewish culture, but also the nature of the J writer's Yahweh himself. It is absurd to think of Yahweh as having mere authority. He is no Roman godling who augments human activities, nor a Homeric god helping to constitute an audience for human heroism.

Yahweh is neither a founder nor an onlooker, though sometimes he can be mistaken for either or both. His essential trope is fatherhood rather than foundation, and his interventions are those of a covenanter rather than of a spectator. You cannot found an authority upon him, because his benignity is manifested not through augmentation but through creation. He does not write; he speaks, and he is heard, in time, and what he continues to create by his speaking is *olam*, time without boundaries, which is more than just an augmentation. More of anything else can come through authority, but more life is the blessing itself, and comes, beyond authority, to Abraham, to Jacob, and to David. No more than Yahweh, do any of them have mere authority. Yet Kafka certainly does have literary authority, and in a troubled way his literary authority is now spiritual also, particularly in Jewish contexts. I do not think that this is a post-Holocaust phenomenon, though Jewish Gnosticism, oxymoronic as it may or may not be, certainly seems appropriate to our time, to many among us. Literary Gnosticism does not seem to me a time-bound phenomenon, anyway. Kafka's *The Castle*, as Erich Heller has argued, is clearly more Gnostic than normative in is spiritual temper, but then so is Shakespeare's *Macbeth*, and Blake's *The Four Zoas*, and Carlyle's *Sartor Resartus*. We sense a Jewish element in Kafka's apparent Gnosticism, even if we are less prepared than Scholem was to name it as a new Kabbalah. In his 1922 Diaries, Kafka subtly insinuated that even his espousal of the Negative was dialectical:

> The Negative alone, however strong it may be, cannot suffice, as in my unhappiest moments I believe it can. For if I have gone the tiniest step upward, won any, be it the most dubious kind of security for myself, I then stretch out on my step and wait for the Negative, not to climb up to me, indeed, but to drag me down from it. Hence it is a defensive instinct in me that won't

tolerate my having the slightest degree of lasting ease and smashes
the marriage bed, for example, even before it has been set up.

What is the Kafkan Negative, whether in this passage or elsewhere?
Let us begin by dismissing the Gallic notion that there is anything Hegelian
about it, any more than there is anything Hegelian about the Freudian
Verneinung. Kafka's Negative, unlike Freud's, is uneasily and remotely
descended from the ancient tradition of negative theology, and perhaps even
from that most negative of ancient theologies, Gnosticism, and yet Kafka,
despite his yearnings for transcendence, joins Freud in accepting the ultimate
authority of the fact. The given suffers no destruction in Kafka or in Freud,
and this given essentially is the way things are, for everyone, and for the
Jews in particular. If fact is supreme, then the mediation of the Hegelian
Negative becomes an absurdity, and no destructive use of such a Negative
is possible, which is to say that Heidegger becomes impossible, and Derrida,
who is a strong misreading of Heidegger, becomes quite unnecessary.

The Kafkan Negative most simply is his Judaism, which is to say the
spiritual form of Kafka's self-conscious Jewishness, as exemplified in that
extraordinary aphorism: "What is laid upon us is to accomplish the negative;
the positive is already given." The positive here is the Law or normative
Judaism; the negative is not so much Kafka's new Kabalah, as it is that which
is still laid upon us: the Judaism of the Negative, of the future as it is always
rushing towards us.

His best biographer to date, Ernst Pawel, emphasizes Kafka's consciousness "of his identity as a Jew, not in the religious, but in the national
sense." Still, Kafka was not a Zionist, and perhaps he longed not so much
for Zion as for a Jewish language, be it Yiddish or Hebrew. He could not
see that his astonishing stylistic purity in German was precisely his way of
not betraying his self-identity as a Jew. In his final phase, Kafka thought of
going to Jerusalem, and again intensified his study of Hebrew. Had he lived,
he would probably have gone to Zion, perfected a vernacular Hebrew, and
given us the bewilderment of Kafkan parables and stories in the language
of the J writer and of Judah Halevi.

V

What calls out for interpretation in Kafka is his refusal to be interpreted,
his evasiveness even in the realm of his own Negative. Two of his most
beautifully enigmatical performances, both late, are the parable, "The Problem
of Our Laws," and the story or testament "Josephine the Singer and the Mouse
Folk." Each allows a cognitive return of Jewish cultural memory, while

refusing the affective identification that would make either parable or tale specifically Jewish in either historical or contemporary identification. "The Problem of Our Laws" is set as a problem in the parable's first paragraph:

> Our laws are not generally known; they are kept secret by the small group of nobles who rule us. We are convinced that these ancient laws are scrupulously administered; nevertheless it is an extremely painful thing to be ruled by laws that one does not know. I am not thinking of possible discrepancies that may arise in the interpretation of the laws, or of the disadvantages involved when only a few and not the whole people are allowed to have a say in their interpretation. These disadvantages are perhaps of no great importance. For the laws are very ancient; their interpretation has been the work of centuries, and has itself doubtless acquired the status of law; and though there is still a possible freedom of interpretation left, it has now become very restricted. Moreover the nobles have obviously no cause to be influenced in their interpretation by personal interests inimical to us, for the laws were made to the advantage of the nobles from the very beginning, they themselves stand above the laws, and that seems to be why the laws were entrusted exclusively into their hands. Of course, there is wisdom in that—who doubts the wisdom of the ancient laws?—but also hardship for us; probably that is unavoidable.

In Judaism, the Law is precisely what is generally known, proclaimed, and taught by the normative sages. The Kabbalah was secret doctrine, but increasingly was guarded not by the normative rabbis, but by Gnostic sectaries, Sabbatarians, and Frankists, all of them ideologically descended from Nathan of Gaza, Sabbatai Zvi's prophet. Kafka twists askew the relations between normative and esoteric Judaism, again making a synecdochal representation impossible. It is not the rabbis or normative sages who stand above the Torah but the *minim*, the heretics from Elisha ben Abuyah through to Jacob Frank, and in some sense, Gershom Scholem as well. To these Jewish Gnostics, as the parable goes on to insinuate: "The Law is whatever the nobles do." So radical a definition tells us "that the tradition is far from complete," and that a kind of messianic expectation is therefore necessary.

> This view, so comfortless as far as the present is concerned, is lightened only by the belief that a time will eventually come when the tradition and our research into it will jointly reach their conclusion, and as it were gain a breathing space, when everything

will have become clear, the law will belong to the people, and the nobility will vanish.

If the parable at this point were to be translated into early Christian terms, then "the nobility" would be the Pharisees, and "the people" would be the Christian believers. But Kafka moves rapidly to stop such a translation: "This is not maintained in any spirit of hatred against the nobility; not at all, and by no one. We are more inclined to hate ourselves, because we have not yet shown ourselves worthy of being entrusted with the laws."

"We" here cannot be either Christians or Jews. Who then are those who "have not yet shown ourselves worthy of being entrusted with the laws"? They would appear to be the crows or jackdaws again, a Kafka or a Hunter Gracchus, wandering about in a state perhaps vulnerable to self-hatred or self-distrust, waiting for a Torah that will not be revealed. Audaciously, Kafka then concludes with overt paradox:

> Actually one can express the problem only in a sort of paradox: Any party that would repudiate not only all belief in the laws, but the nobility as well, would have the whole people behind it; yet no such party can come into existence, for nobody would dare to repudiate the nobility. We live on this razor's edge. A writer once summed the matter up in this way: The sole visible and indubitable law that is imposed upon us is the nobility, and must we ourselves deprive ourselves of that one law?

Why would no one dare to repudiate the nobility, whether we read them as normative Pharisees, Jewish Gnostic heresiarchs, or whatever? Though imposed upon us, the sages or the minim are the only visible evidence of law that we have. Who are we then? How is the parable's final question, whether open or rhetorical, to be answered? "Must we ourselves deprive ourselves of that one law?" Blake's answer, in The Marriage of Heaven and Hell, was: "One Law for the Lion and the Ox is Oppression." But what is one law for the crows? Kafka will not tell us whether it is oppression or not.

Josephine the singer also is a crow or Kafka, rather than a mouse, and the folk may be interpreted as an entire nation of jackdaws. The spirit of the Negative, dominant if uneasy in "The Problem of Our Laws," is loosed into a terrible freedom in Kafka's testamentary story. That is to say: in the parable, the laws could not be Torah, though that analogue flickered near. But in Josephine's story, the mouse folk simultaneously are and are not the Jewish people, and Franz Kafka both is and is not their curious singer. Cognitively the identifications are possible, as though returned from forgetfulness, but affectively they certainly are not, unless we can assume that crucial aspects making up the identifications have been purposefully, if other than consciously, forgotten. Josephine's piping *is* Kafka's story, and yet Kafka's story is hardly Josephine's piping.

Can there be a mode of negation neither conscious nor unconscious, neither Hegelian nor Freudian? Kafka's genius provides one, exposing many shades between consciousness and the work of repression, many demarcations far ghostlier than we could have imagined without him. Perhaps the ghostliest come at the end of the story:

> Josephine's road, however, must go downhill. The time will soon come when her last notes sound and die into silence. She is a small episode in the eternal history of our people, and the people will get over the loss of her. Not that it will be easy for us; how can our gatherings take place in utter silence? Still, were they not silent even when Josephine was present? Was her actual piping notably louder and more alive than the memory of it will be? Was it even in her lifetime more than a simply memory? Was it not rather because Josephine's singing was already past losing in this way that our people in their wisdom prized it so highly?
>
> So perhaps we shall not miss so very much after all, while Josephine, redeemed from the earthly sorrows which to her thinking lay in wait for all chosen spirits, will happily lose herself in the numberless throng of the heroes of our people, and soon, since we are no historians, will rise to the heights of redemption and be forgotten like all her brothers.

"I am a Memory come alive," Kafka wrote in the Diaries. Whether or not he intended it, he was Jewish memory come alive. "Was it even in her lifetime more than a simple memory?" Kafka asks, knowing that he too was past losing. The Jews are no historians, in some sense, because Jewish memory, as Yosef Yerushalmi has demonstrated, is a normative mode and not a historical one. Kafka, if he could have prayed, might have prayed to rise to the heights of redemption and be forgotten like most of his brothers and sisters. But his prayer would not have been answered. When we think of *the* Catholic writer, we think of Dante, who nevertheless had the audacity to enshrine his Beatrice in the hierarchy of Paradise. If we think of *the* Protestant writer, we think of Milton, a party or sect of one, who believed that the soul was mortal, and would be resurrected only in conjunction with the body. Think of *the* Jewish writer, and you must think of Kafka, who evaded his own audacity, and believed nothing, and trusted only in the Covenant of being a writer.

VI

What can it mean to trust in the Covenant, not between Yahweh and the Jewish people, but between writing and a writer? Gregor Samsa is a solitary (his last name, in Czech, can be translated "I am alone"), a commercial traveller, and a kind of family pariah or outcast, at least in his own tormented vision. His celebrated metamorphosis, into a kind of huge bedbug, is completed in the story's first sentence. Gregor's fate is certain but without hope; there is plenty of hope, for writing as for God, but none for Gregor. The Law, which is the way things are, including one's parents' huge debt to one's employer, is essentially a universal compulsion to repeat. No irony, however well handled, can represent repetition compulsion as the Law of the Jews. Samsa's employer is therefore not Yahweh, but another version of the Gnostic Demiurge, ruler of the cosmological emptiness in which we dwell.

The only rage to order that Kafka knew was his implicit rage not to be interpreted. There can be no ultimate coherence to my Gnostic interpretation (nor to Scholem's, nor Benjamin's, nor Heller's, nor to anyone's) because Kafka refuses the Gnostic quest for the alien God, for one's own spark or *pneuma* rejoining the original Abyss somewhere out of this world. The huge bedbug is neither the fallen husk of Samsa nor his potentially saving *pneuma*. It can hardly be his spark from the original Abyss because it is a horrible vermin, and yet only after his transformation into a bug is Gregor capable of aesthetic apprehension. Like Shakespeare's grotesque Caliban, the insect Samsa hears the beautiful in music, and so for the first time apprehends another sphere. Kafka refused an illustration for *The Metamorphosis* that would have portrayed Gregor Samsa as a literal beetle or bedbug: "The insect itself cannot be drawn. It cannot be drawn even as if seen from a distance." This is not to say that Samsa suffers an hallucination, but only reminds us that a negation cannot be visually represented, which in turn reminds us of Kafkan nostalgias for the Second Commandment.

Is Gregor accurate in his final consciousness that his death is a liberation, an act of love for his family? Wilhelm Emrich, elsewhere so wary a Kafka exegete, fell into this momentary passion for the positive, an entrapment all readers of Kafka suffer sooner or later, so exhausted are we by this greatest master of evasions. Because the insect is inexplicable, it does not necessarily contain any truth. *The Metamorphosis*, like all crucial Kafkan narratives, takes place somewhere *between* truth and meaning, a "somewhere" identical with the modern Jewish rupture from the normative tradition. Truth is in hope and neither is available to us, while meaning is in the future or the messianic age, and we will not come up to either. We are lazy, but industry will not avail us either, not even the industrious zeal with which every writer prides himself upon accepting his own death. If *The Metamorphosis* is a satire, then it is self-satire, or post-Nietzschean parody, that humiliates Kafka's only covenant, the placing of trust in the transcendental possibility of being a strong writer.

The story then cannot be interpreted coherently as a fantasy of death and resurrection, or as an allegory on the less-is-more fate of being a writer. Gregor's death is not an effectual sacrifice, not a self-fulfillment, and not even a tragic irony of any kind. It is another Kafkan negation that refuses to negate the given, which is the world of Freud's reality principle. Gregor does not become a child again as he dies. Yet we cannot even call him a failure, which might guarantee his upward fall to the heights of redemption. Like Gracchus, like the bucket-rider, like the country doctor, like the hunger artist, Gregor is suspended between the truth of the past, or Jewish memory, and the meaning of the future, or Jewish messianism. Poor Gregor therefore evades the categories both of belief and of poetry. How much would most of us know about this rupture without Kafka, or Kafka's true heir, Beckett?

A Gnosticism without transcendence is not a knowing but is something else, and there is no transcendence in the *Metamorphosis*, or anywhere in Kafka. To transcend in a world of rupture you only need to change your direction, but that is to adopt the stance of the cat (or Gnostic archon) of Kafka's magnificent and appalling parable, "A Little Fable":

> "Alas," said the mouse, "the world is growing smaller every day. At the beginning it was so big that I was afraid, I kept running and running, and I was glad when at last I saw walls far away to the right and left, but these long walls have narrowed so quickly that I am in the last chamber already, and there in the corner stands the trap that I must run into." "You only need to change your direction," said the cat, and ate it up.
>
> (Translated by Willa and Edwin Muir)

Gregor Samsa and Modern Spirituality

Martin Greenberg

> *The mother follow'd, weeping loud,*
> *'O, that I such a fiend should bear!"*
> BLAKE

> *In the Middle Ages it was the temporal which was the inessential in relation to sprituality;*
> *in the nineteenth century the opposite occurred: the temporal was primary and the spiritual*
> *was the inessential parasite which gnawed away at it and tried to destroy it.*
> SARTRE

The Metamorphosis is peculiar as a narrative in having its climax in the very first sentence: "As Gregor Samsa awoke one morning from uneasy dreams he found himself transformed in his bed into a gigantic insect." The rest of the novella falls away from this high point of astonishment in one long expiring sigh, punctuated by three subclimaxes (the three eruptions of the bug from the bedroom). How is it possible, one may ask, for a story to start at the climax and then merely subside? What kind of story is that? The answer to this question is, I think: A story for which the traditional Aristotelian form of narrative (complication and denouement) has lost any intrinsic necessity and which has therefore evolved its own peculiar form out of the very matter it seeks to tell. *The Metamorphosis* produces its form out of itself. The traditional kind of narrative based on the drama of denouement—on the "unknotting" of complications and the coming to a conclusion—could not serve Kafka because it is just exactly the absence of denouement and conclusions that is his subject matter. His story is about death, but death that is without denouement, death that is merely a spiritually inconclusive petering out.

From *The Terror of Art: Kafka and Modern Literature.* © 1965 by Martin Greenberg. Basic Books, 1965.

The first sentence of *The Metamorphosis* announces Gregor Samsa's death and the rest of the story is his slow dying. In its movement as an inexorable march toward death it resembles Tolstoy's *Death of Ivan Ilyich*. As Ivan Ilyich struggles against the knowledge of his own death, so does Gregor Samsa. But Tolstoy's work is about death literally and existentially; Kafka's is about death in life. Until Ivan Ilyich stops defending his life to himself as a good one and recognizes that it has not been what it ought to have been, he cannot accept the knowledge that he is dying; finally he embraces the truth of his life, which is at the same time the truth of death, and discovers spiritual light and life as he dies. Kafka's protagonist also struggles against "the truths of life and death"; in Gregor Samsa's case, however, his life is his death and there is no salvation. For a moment, it is true, near the end of his long dying, while listening to his sister play the violin, he feels "as if the way were opening before him to the unknown nourishment he craved"; but the nourishment remains unknown, he is locked into his room for the last time and he expires.

What Gregor awakens to on the morning of his metamorphosis is the truth of his life. His ordinary consciousness has lied to him about himself; the explosive first sentence pitches him out of the lie of his habitual self-understanding into the nightmare of truth. "The dream reveals the reality" of his abasement and self-abasement by a terrible metaphor; he is vermin (*Ungeziefer*), a disgusting creature (or rather uncreature) shut out from "the human circle." The poetic of the Kafka story, based on the dream, requires the literal assertion of metaphor; Gregor must literally *be* vermin. This gives Kafka's representation of the subjective reality its convincing vividness. Anything less than metaphor, such as a simile comparing Gregor to vermin, would diminish the reality of what he is trying to represent. Gregor's thinking "What has happened to me? . . . It was no dream," is no contradiction of his metamorphosis' being a dream but a literal-ironical confirmation of it. Of course it is no dream—to the dreamer. The dreamer, while he is dreaming, takes his dream as real; Gregor's thought is therefore literally true to the circumstances in which he finds himself. However, it is also true ironically, since his metamorphosis is indeed no dream (meaning something unreal) but a revelation of the truth.

What, then, is the truth of Gregor's life? There is first of all his soul-destroying job, which keeps him on the move and cuts him off from the possibility of real human associations:

> Oh God, he thought, what an exhausting job I've picked on! Traveling about day in, day out. It's much more irritating work than doing the actual business in the office, and on top of that

there's the trouble of constant traveling, of worrying about train
connections, the bad and irregular meals, the human associations
that are no sooner struck up than they are ended without ever
becoming intimate. The devil take it all!

Not only is his work lonely and exhausting, it is also degrading. Gregor
fails to report to work once in five years and the chief clerk is at his home
at a quarter past seven in the morning accusing him of neglect of his business
duties, poor work in general and stealing company funds, and threatening
him with dismissal. In the guilt-world that Gregor inhabits, his missing his
train on this one morning retroactively changes his excellent work record
at one stroke into the very opposite.

What a fate, to be condemned to work for a firm where the
smallest omission at once gave rise to the gravest suspicion! Were
all employees in a body nothing but scoundrels?

He has been sacrificing himself by working at his meaningless, degrading
job so as to pay off an old debt of his parents' to his employer. Otherwise
"I'd have given notice long ago, I'd have gone to the chief and told him
exactly what I think of him." But even now, with the truth of his self-betrayal
pinning him on his back to his bed, he is unable to claim himself for himself
and decide to quit — he must wait "another five or six years":

[O]nce I've saved enough money to pay back my parents' debts
to him — that should take another five or six years — I'll go it without fail. I'll cut myself completely loose then. For the moment,
though, I'd better get up, since my train goes at five.

He pretends that he will get up and resume his old life. He will get dressed
"and above all eat his breakfast," after which the "morning's delusions" will
infallibly be dissipated. But the human self whose claims he always post-
poned and continues to postpone, is past being put off, having declared itself
negatively by changing him from a human being into an insect. His metamorphosis is a judgment on himself by his defeated humanity.

Gregor's humanity has been defeated in his private life as much as in
his working life. His mother succinctly describes its deathly aridity as she
pleads with the chief clerk:

"[H]e's not well, sir, believe me. What else would make him
miss a train! The boy thinks about nothing but his work. It makes
me almost cross the way he never goes out in the evenings; he's

been here the last eight days and has stayed at home every single evening. He just sits there quietly at the table reading a newspaper or looking through railway timetables. The only amusement he gets is doing fretwork. For instance, he spent two or three evenings cutting out a little picture frame; you would be surprised to see how pretty it is; it's hanging in his room; you'll see it in a minute when Gregor opens the door."

The picture in the little frame shows a woman in furs "holding out to the spectator a huge fur muff into which the whole of her forearm had vanished"; it is the second object that Gregor's eye encounters when he surveys his room on waking (the first was his collection of samples). Later in the story, when his sister and mother empty his room of its furniture, he defends his "human past" by making his stand on this picture, pressing "himself to the glass, which was a good surface to hold on to and comforted his hot belly." That is about what Gregor's "human past" amounts to: a pin-up.

For most of the story, Gregor struggles with comic-terrible pathos against the metaphor fastened on him. His first hope is that it is all "nonsense." But he cannot tell; the last thing he knows about is himself. So he works himself into an upright position in order to unlock the door, show himself to the chief clerk and his family, and let them decide for him, as he has always let others decide for him:

> If they were horrified then the responsibility was no longer his and he could stay quiet. But if they took it calmly, then he had no reason either to be upset, and could really get to the station for the eight o'clock train if he hurried.

The answer that he gets is his mother's swoon, the chief clerk's hurried departure, in silent-movie style, with a loud "Ugh!" and his father's driving him back "pitilessly," with a newspaper and a walking stick that menaces his life, into his room — "from behind his father gave him a strong push which was literally a deliverance and he flew far into the room, bleeding freely. The door was slammed behind him with the stick, and then at last there was silence."

This is the first repulse the metamorphosed Gregor suffers in his efforts to reenter "the human circle." The fact that his voice has altered so that the others can no longer understand what he says, but he can understand them as well as ever, perfectly expresses the pathos of one who is condemned to stand on the outside looking in. Although he must now accept the fact that he has been changed into a monster, he clings to the illusion that his new state is a temporary one: "he must lie low for the present and, by exercising patience and the utmost consideration, help the family to bear the inconvenience he was bound to cause them in his present condition." Like Ivan Ilyich, he wants to believe that his mortal illness is only a "condition."

In part 2 we learn about Gregor's all-important relations with his family. An unambiguous indication already given in part 1 is the fact that he locks his bedroom doors at night "even at home"—a "prudent habit he had acquired in traveling." Although he is a dutiful, self-sacrificing son, just such a dutiful son as Georg Bendemann, he is as much a stranger to his family as he is to the world and shuts them out of his life—he locks them out as much as they lock him in. Concealment, mistrust, and denial mark the relations in the Samsa family. It now turns out, as Gregor listens at his bedroom door, that some investments had survived the wreck of Samsa Sr.'s business five years before and had even increased since then, though he thought his father had been left with nothing, "at least his father had never said anything to the contrary, and of course he had not asked him directly." Moreover, this sum had been increased by the unexpended residue of Gregor's earnings, who "kept only a few dollars for himself." But he buries the rage he feels at this evidence of the needlessness of his self-sacrifice, as he has always buried his real feelings:

> Gregor nodded his head eagerly, rejoiced at this evidence of unexpected thrift and foresight. True, he could really have paid off some more of his father's debts to the chief with this extra money, and so brought much nearer the day on which he could quit his job, but doubtless it was better the way his father had arranged it.

His parents liked to think that his slaving at his job to support the family represented no sacrifice of himself—"they had convinced themselves in the course of years that Gregor was settled for life in this firm." But they were able to convince themselves of this only because he himself cooperated eagerly with them to deny himself. Deception and self-deception, denial and self-denial now "end in horror." To cap it all, it turns out that his family did not even need his sacrifice for another reason: When Gregor ceases to be the breadwinner, father, mother, and sister all turn to and provide for themselves and the old man is even rescued in this way from a premature dotage.

The decisive figure in the family for Gregor is his father. He sees him something like Georg Bendemann saw his—as an old man, almost a doddering old man, and yet strong. This combination of weakness and strength is signaled in the story's very first words about Samsa Sr.: "at one of the side doors his father was knocking, gently [*schwach:* weakly], yet with his fist." The combination is present in the description of the father's response to Gregor's first breaking out of his boredom—a "knotted fist" and "fierce expression" go along with tears of helplessness and humiliation:

> His father knotted his fist with a fierce expression on his face as if he meant to knock Gregor back into his room, then looked uncertainly round the living room, covered his eyes with his hands and wept till his great chest [*mächtige Brust*] heaved.

But in spite of his "great chest," in spite of his voice's sounding "no longer like the voice of one single father" when he drives his son back into his room, in spite of Gregor's being "dumbfounded at the enormous size of his shoe soles," the second time his father chases him back into his room, the elder Samsa, unlike the elder Bendemann, does not loom large like a Titanic figure. He is powerful, irascible and petulant, but not mythically powerful. His shoe soles seem "enormous" to his son because of his insect angle of vision—not because the old man is superhuman but because the son is less than human. Everything in the story is seen from Gregor's point of view, the point of view of somebody who has fallen below the human level.

The father's strength is the ordinary strength of human life, which has been temporarily dimmed by his business failure and his son's unnatural ascendancy as the breadwinner of the family. He does not battle his son to recover his ascendancy as Bendemann Sr. does in "The Judgment." There is no battle; Gregor cannot "risk standing up to him." The unnatural state of affairs in the Samsa home corrects itself so to speak naturally, by the son's showing forth as what he really is—a parasite that saps the father's and the family's life. A fundamental incompatibility exists between the son and the family, between sickliness and parasitism on the one hand and vigor and independence on the other, between death and life. As the son's life wanes the family's revives; especially the father's flourishes with renewed vigor and he becomes a blustering, energetic, rather ridiculous man—a regular Kafka papa.

From the start Gregor's father deals brutally with him:

> [F]rom the very first day of his new life . . . his father believed only the severest measures suitable for dealing with him.

Indeed he threatens his life: the first time he shoos Gregor back into his room he menaces him with a "fatal blow" from his stick; at his son's second outbreak he gives him a wound from which he never recovers. But though Samsa Sr. throws his son back into his room two out of the three times he breaks out of it, Gregor's banishment from "the human circle" is not a sentence passed on him by his father. Unlike the father in "The Judgment," Samsa Sr. does not stand at the center of the story confronting his son as the lord and judge of his life. He stands with the mother and the sister, opposite the son but to the side; the center of the story is completely occupied by the son. The father affirms the judgment passed on Gregor—that he is "unfit for life"—but the judgment is not his; it is Gregor's. At the beginning of the novella, before he is locked in his room by the family as a metamorphosed monster, we see how he has already locked himself in as a defeated human being. Gregor is self-condemned.

At the side of the father stands the mother, gentle ("That gentle voice!"), yet "in complete union with him" against her son. Gregor's monstrousness horrifies her no less than the others and she faints at the sight of him. For the first two weeks she prefers, with the father, not to know how or even if Gregor is fed. "Not that they would have wanted him to starve, of course, but perhaps they could not have borne to know more about his feeding than from hearsay."—Gregor's struggle, in these words, against the truth is a pathetically ironical statement of it. Frau Samsa pities her son—"he is my unfortunate son"—and understands his plight as illness; the morning of the metamorphosis she sends the daughter for the doctor, while Herr Samsa, characteristically (his son is a recalcitrant creature bent on causing him a maximum of annoyance), sends the maid for the locksmith. (Gregor, feeling "himself drawn once more into the human circle" by these steps, "hoped for great and remarkable results from both the doctor and the locksmith, without really distinguishing precisely between them"—agreeing with both parents, he is unable to distinguish between the element of recalcitrance and refusal and the element of illness in his withdrawal into inhuman isolation.) Shame and horror, however, overwhelm the mother's compassion—we learn from Gregor's reflections that the doctor was sent away on some pretext. She protests against Grete's clearing the furniture out of Gregor's room— "Doesn't it look as if we were showing him, by taking away his furniture, that we have given up hope of his ever getting better?"—but then acquiesces weakly in it and even helps to move the heavy pieces. At the end, when Grete says that the bug must be got rid of:

> "He must go," cried Gregor's sister, "that's the only solution, Father. You must just try to get rid of the idea that this is Gregor. . . . If this were Gregor, he would have realized long ago that human beings can't live with such a creature, and he'd have gone away on his own accord."

the mother, with a terrible silence, acquiesces again in her daughter's determination, which this time is a condemnation of her son to death.

Gregor cherishes his sister most of all. She in turn shows the most awareness of his needs after his metamorphosis into vermin and he is grateful to her for it. But he notices that she avoids touching anything that has come into contact with him and he is forced to "realize how repulsive the sight of him still was to her, and that it was bound to go on being repulsive." For her, too, he is a pariah, a monster shut out of the human circle, and at the end she is the one who voices the thought, which has hung unexpressed over the family since the morning of the metamorphosis, that Gregor must be got rid of.

This, then, is the situation in the Samsa family revealed by the metamorphosis: on the surface, the official sentiments of the parents and the sister toward Gregor, and of Gregor toward them and toward himself; underneath, the horror and disgust, and self-disgust: "family duty required the suppression of disgust and the exercise of patience, nothing but patience."

Gregor breaks out of his room the first time hoping that his transformation will turn out to be "nonsense"; the second time, in the course of defending at least his hope of returning to his "human past." His third eruption, in part 3, has quite a different aim. The final section of the story discovers a Gregor who tries to dream again, after a long interval, of resuming his old place at the head of the family, but the figures from the past that now appear to him—his boss, the chief clerk, traveling salesmen, a chambermaid ("a sweet and fleeting memory"), and so on—cannot help him, "they were one and all unapproachable and he was glad when they vanished." Defeated, he finally gives up all hope of returning to the human community. Now his existence slopes steeply toward death. The wound in his back, made by the apple his father threw at him in driving Gregor back into his room after his second outbreak, has begun to fester again; his room is now the place in which all the household's dirty old decayed things are thrown, along with Gregor, a dirty old decayed thing; and he has just about stopped eating.

At first he had thought he was unable to eat out of "chagrin over the state of his room"—his mood at that stage of his dying, like Ivan Ilyich's at a corresponding stage, was one of hatred toward his family for neglecting him; he hissed at them all in rage. But then he discovered that he got "increasing enjoyment" from crawling about the filth and junk—it was not the filthiness of his room that was preventing him from eating. On the last evening of his life, watching from his room the lodgers whom his family have taken in putting away a good supper, he comes to a crucial realization:

"I'm hungry enough." said Gregor sadly to himself, "but not for that kind of food. How these lodgers are stuffing themselves, and here am I dying of starvation!"

In giving up at last all hope of reentering the human circle, Gregor finally understands the truth about his life; which is to say he accepts the knowledge of his death, for the truth about his life is his death-in-life by his banishment and self-banishment from the human community. But having finally accepted the truth, having finally bowed to the yoke of the metaphor that he has been trying to shake off, he begins to sense a possibility that exists for him *only* in his outcast state. He is hungry enough, he realizes, but not for the world's fare, "not for that kind of food." He feels a hunger that can only be felt in full acceptance of his outcast state. Like Ivan Ilyich when he accepts his death at last and plunges into the black sack's hole, he perceives a glimmer of light; in the degradation, in the utter negativity of his outcastness, he begins to apprehend a positive possibility.

He has already had a hint or two that the meaning of his metamorphosis contains some sort of positive possibility. At the beginning of the story, when he is lying in bed and worrying about not reporting to work, he thinks of saying he is sick, but knows that the sick-insurance doctor will come down on him as a malingerer. "And would he be so far from wrong on this occasion? Gregor really felt quite well . . . and he was even unusually hungry." He has just been changed into a huge bug and he is afraid of pleading sick because he will be accused of malingering! And the accusation would after all be correct because he felt quite well and was even unusually hungry! "Of course," the reader says, "he means quite well *as an insect!*" — which is a joke, but a joke that points right to the positive meaning of his metamorphosis.

A second hint soon follows. After Gregor unlocks the bedroom door with his jaws and drops down on his legs for the first time, he experiences "a sense of physical comfort; his legs had firm ground under them; . . . they even strove to carry him forward in whatever direction he chose; and he was inclined to believe that a final relief from all his sufferings was at hand." The first meaning here is ironical and comic: Gregor, unable to accept his transformation into a bug and automatically trying to walk like a man, inadvertently falls down on his insect legs and feels an instantaneous sense of comfort which he takes as a promise of future relief from his sufferings. With supreme illogic he derives a hope of release from his animal condition from the very comfort he gets by adapting himself to that condition — so divided is his self-consciousness from his true self. But there is a second meaning, which piles irony upon the irony; *precisely* as a noisome outcast from the human world Gregor feels the possibility of relief, of *final* relief. *Only* as an outcast does he sense the possibility of an ultimate salvation rather than just a restoration of the status quo.

As a bug, too, his wounds heal a lot faster than did his old cut finger: the vitality possible to him in his pariah state (if he can only find the food he needs to feed his spiritual hunger on, for he is "unusually hungry") is in sharp contrast with his human debility. And he finds a kind of freedom in crawling around the walls and ceiling of his room instead of going to work each morning—Kafka dwells so much in the first part on the horror of Samsa's job that we feel his metamorphosis as something of a liberation, although in the end he is only delivered from the humiliation and death of his job into the humiliation and death of his outcast state.

When Gregor breaks out of his room the third and last time, he is no longer trying to deceive himself about himself and get back to his old life with its illusions about belonging to the human community. He is trying to find that "final relief" which lies beyond "the last earthly frontier," a frontier which is to be approached only through exile and solitude. What draws him out of his room the last night of his life is his sister's violin playing. Although he had never cared for music in his human state, now the notes of the violin attract him surprisingly. Indifferent to "his growing lack of consideration for the others"—at last he has the courage to think about himself—trailing "fluff and hair and remnants of food" which he no longer bothers to scrape off himself, the filthy starving underground creature advances onto "the spotless floor of the living room" where his sister is playing for the three lodgers.

> Was he an animal, that music had such an effect upon him? He felt as if the way were opening before him to the unknown nourishment he craved.

It is a familiar Romantic idea that Kafka is making use of here: that music expresses the inexpressible, that it points to a hidden sphere of spiritual power and meaning. It is only in his extremity, as "an animal," an outcast from human life who finally accepts his being cast out, that Gregor's ears are opened to music. Yet in spite of all the hints he has had, Gregor still hesitates to grasp the positive possibility contained in the truth about himself and his death in life—the possibility of life in death, of spiritual life through outcastness. All along he has understood the well-being he feels as an insect as an indication of his bestialization. "Am I less sensitive now?" he asks himself after marveling at his recuperative powers as a bug; he accuses himself of a growing lack of consideration for others, and so on. Now he does the same thing: "Was he an animal, that music had such an effect upon him?" This time, however, his understanding of himself is clearly a misunderstanding; it is nonsensical to associate music and bestiality, music is at the opposite pole from bestiality. His metamorphosis is a path to the spiritual rather than the bestial. The violin notes that move him so build a way through his death in life to the salvation for which he blindly hungers.

Or they only seem to. Certainly the unknown nourishment exists; the goal of his hunger exists. But the music merely draws him toward his sister with the jealous intention of capturing her for himself and immuring her in his cell with him; it only leads him out into the same old living room of his death as a private person, which with the three indignant lodgers staring down at him is the same old public world of bullying businessmen he knew as a traveling salesman (Heinz Politzer, *Franz Kafka: Parable and Paradox*). "There is a goal, but no way," Kafka says in one of his aphorisms; "what we call a way is only wavering."

His final repulse follows, with his sister demanding that "he must go. . . . If this were Gregor, he would have realized long ago that human beings can't live with such a creature." Painfully turning around, Gregor crawls back into his room without his father's having to chase him back and surrenders his life to this demand:

> "And what now?" said Gregor to himself, looking round in the darkness. . . . He thought of his family with tenderness and love. The decision that he must disappear was one that he held to even more strongly than his sister, if that were possible. In this state of vacant and peaceful mediation he remained until the tower clock struck three in the morning. The first broadening of light in the world outside the window entered his consciousness once more. Then his head sank to the floor of its own accord and from his nostrils came the last faint flicker of his breath.

Both Georg Bendemann and Gregor Samsa die reconciled with their families in a tenderness of self-condemnation. But Georg is sentenced to death by his father; nobody sentences Gregor to his death in life except himself. His ultimate death, however, his death without redemption, is from hunger for the unknown nourishment he needs. What kills Gregor is spiritual starvation — "Man cannot live without a permanent trust in something indestructible in himself, and at the same time that indestructible something as well as his trust in it may remain permanently concealed from him."

Although the story does not end with Gregor's death, it is still from his point of view that the last few pages are narrated. The family are of course glad to be freed of the burden and scandal he has been to them but dare not say so openly. When the tough old charwoman who has survived "the worst a long life could offer" spares them the embarrassment of getting "rid of the thing," their thanks is to fire her. However the tide of life, now flooding in, soon sweeps them beyond bad conscience and troubled reflections. They make a holiday of Gregor's death day and take a trolley ride into the country. Spring is in the air; a review of their prospects shows them to be "not at all bad." Mother and father notice how their daughter, in spite of everything, has

> bloomed into a pretty girl with a good figure. They grew quieter and half unconsciously exchanged glances of complete agreement, having come to the conclusion that it would soon be time to find a good husband for her. And it was like a confirmation of their new dreams and excellent intentions that at the end of their journey their daughter sprang to her feet first and stretched her young body.

Life triumphs blatantly, not only over Gregor's unlife but over his posthumous irony — these last lines are entirely without irony. Or if they are ironical, it is at Gregor's expense: his moral condemnation of his family here turns into a condemnation of himself. Kafka got his peroration from a description of Ivan Ilyich's daughter in Tolstoy's story, only he twists its meaning right around:

> His daughter came in all dressed up, with much of her young body naked, making a show of it, while his body was causing him such torture. She was strong and healthy, evidently very much in love, and annoyed that his illness and suffering and death should cast a shadow upon her happiness.

Tolstoy's condemnation of the living, with their vulgar bursting vitality and impatience to get on with their business of living forever, in Kafka's hands becomes life's impatient condemnation of the dead that is the novella's last word: "We are sinful not merely because we have eaten of the Tree of Knowledge, but also because we have not yet eaten of the Tree of Life. The state in which we find ourselves is sinful, quite independent of guilt."

Tolstoy's story is dramatic, with a reversal (peripety) and a denouement at the end in which the dying man finds salvation and death is no more. In Kafka's story there is the beginning of a reversal when Gregor thinks the way to unknown nourishment is opening before him, but it fails to take place and the novella sinks to the conclusion that has been implicit in it from the start. Kafka's story has little drama; a climax that occurs in the first sentence is no real climax. At the beginning of the chapter I described this nondramatic movement of *The Metamorphosis* as a dying fall, a sinking, an ebbing. *The Trial* and *The Castle* too have more or less the same movement, and in his diary entry of December 13, 1914, Kafka remarks on this dying movement of his best work:

> [T]he best things I have written have their basis in this capacity of mine to die contentedly. All these fine and very convincing passages always deal with the fact that somebody is dying, that it is hard for him to do, that it seems unjust to him or at least cruel, and the reader finds this moving or at least I think he should. For me, however, who believes that I'll be able to lie contentedly on my deathbed, such descriptions are secretly a game, I positively enjoy my own death in the dying person's, therefore I calculatingly exploit the attention that the reader concentrates on death, understand it a lot more clearly than he, who I assume will complain on his deathbed, and for these reasons my complaining [*Klage*, lament] is as perfect as can be, doesn't suddenly break off in the way real complaining is likely to do, but dies away beautifully and purely. It is the same thing as my always complaining to my mother about pains that weren't nearly as bad as my complaints made one think.

The passage is a characteristically ambivalent appreciation and depreciation of his art for the very same reasons. On the side of depreciation, he suggests that his stories aren't real stories at all, with the dramatic conflict of real stories, but a "game" he plays with the reader: behind the apparent struggle of his protagonists to live, undermining and betraying it from the start, is his own secret embrace of death. And just because the struggle is a fake one he is able to prolong it artfully into a sort of swan song, a swan song which at the end of the diary entry he compares to his hypochondriacal complainings to his mother, to his constant whinings about aches and pains. In this Kafka seems to be agreeing with those critics who find him a pusillanimous neurotic, lacking in any force or fight. Edmund Wilson thinks he is "at his most characteristic when he is assimilating men to beasts—dogs, insects, mice, and apes—which can neither dare nor know. . . . the denationalized, discouraged, disaffected, disabled Kafka . . . can in the end only let us down" (*Classics and Commercials*). A psychoanalytic critic concludes that "the striving for synthesis, for integration and harmony which are the marks of a healthy ego and a healthy art are lacking in Kafka's life and in his writings. The conflict is weak in Kafka's stories because the ego is submissive; the unequal forces within the Kafka psyche create no tension within the reader, only a fraternal sadness" (Selma Fraiberg, "Kafka and the Dream").

But on the side of appreciation, Kafka sees his understanding of death as being responsible for his "best things." Thanks to his underlying acceptance of death, the selfsame story that he is always telling about somebody who finds it hard to die is "as perfect as can be" and "dies away beautifully and purely."

Which is it then? Is *The Metamorphosis* unhealthy art — the artfully prolonged whine of a disaffected neurotic with a submissive ego? Or is it a lament (*Klage*) that is perfect, beautiful, pure? Does Kafka let us down in the end or does he try to lift us up "into the pure, the true, the unchangeable" (*The Diaries of Franz Kafka, 1914–1923*, trans. Joseph Kresh)? The two opposing characterizations, "neurotic whine" and "beautiful lament," which I have drawn from Kafka's diary entry express very different judgments, but they agree in pointing to something lyrical about the form of his "best things," something in the nature of a crying-out, rather than a narrative of action with complication and denouement. Doubtless Kafka's critics would find him depressing in any case. Yet in taxing his stories with lack of tension they misunderstand their form and ask them to be what they are not and do not try to be — representations of action. And in missing their form they miss the meaning — these stories do not mean the unmanliness and discouragement of their protagonists; they mean the courage to see the unmanliness and discouragement which live like an infection at the heart of modern spirituality, perhaps even, as Kafka wrote to Milena Jesenská, at the heart of "all faith since the beginning of time."

The Metamorphosis does not unfold an action but a metaphor; it is the spelling out of a metaphor. It does not end in an Aristotelian denouement, but draws the metaphor out to its ultimate conclusion which is death. I called the movement of the story a dying fall. But visual terms serve better than auditory ones. The movement is a seeing more and more: waking up, the metamorphosed Gregor sees his insect belly, then his helplessly waving leg, then his room, cloth samples, picture, alarm clock, furniture, key, living room, family, chief clerk — on and on and on in a relentless march of ever deeper seeing till he sees his own death. Everything he sees is a building stone added to the structure of the metaphor of his banishment from the human circle, capped by the stone of his death. In a story of this kind there is no question of tension or of any of the specifically dramatic qualities: it is a vision.

Of course Gregor Samsa "can neither dare nor know." Neither can Hamlet, his ultimate literary ancestor and the earliest protagonist of the modern theme of doubt and despair in face of the threat of universal meaninglessness. That is just the point of the story: Gregor can neither dare nor know, neither live in the world nor find the unknown truth he craves. The final words of Dostoevsky's Underground Man, commenting on his own *Notes*, are very opposite here:

> [A] novel needs a hero, and all the traits for an antihero are *expressly* gathered together here, and, what matters most, it all produces a most unpleasant impression, for we are all divorced from life, we are all cripples, every one of us, more or less. . . . "Speak for yourself," you say, "and for your miseries in your underground hole, but don't dare to say 'all of us.'" Excuse me, gentlemen, I am not justifying myself with that "all of us." As for what concerns me in particular, I have only carried to an extreme in my life what you have not dared to carry halfway, and, what's more, you have taken your cowardice for good sense, and have found comfort in deceiving yourselves. So that perhaps, after all, there is more life in me than in you. Look into it more carefully! Why, we don't even know what living means now, what it is, and what it is called! Leave us alone without books and we shall be lost and in confusion at once. We shall not know what to join onto, what to cling to, what to love and what to hate, what to respect and what to despise.

What the Underground Man is saying, what he says all along in his *Notes*, is that action and awareness, daring and knowledge, world and spirit are no longer united but split. To act in the world requires life-confidence based on knowledge; but the Underground Man's "overacute consciousness" exposes doubt which undermine his confidence—self-awareness turns him into a "mouse" who is incapable of avenging an affront, a nasty "babbler" who can only sit with folded hands. On the other hand, "all 'direct' persons and men of action are active just because they are stupid and limited." The man of action and the man of consciousness, the man of the world and the man of the spirit are equally failures, equally cripples; the one because he is stupid, and the other because he is ignominious. Neither knows "what living means now, what it is, and what it is called."

Gregor Samsa, not even a mouse but a bug, finds that his sister's violin music draws him with the promise of that knowledge of "what to love and what to hate, what to respect and what to despise" which would make it possible to realize the union of world and spirit. But his effort to penetrate the mystery of such knowledge fails and he surrenders to the impossibility of living.

Does the Underground Man, Dostoevsky's and Kafka's, make his misery out to be the *summum bonum*? Does he end up morbidly affirming his unlife as the highest life? So Lionel Trilling thinks. He finds in the hissings and spittings of the Russian writer's "antihero" a fundamental rejection of the pleasure principle—meaning by pleasure sensual gratification first of all and after that the health of the entire human being as expressed in the energetic use of his powers for the attainment of life-success. Instead the Underground Man chooses suffering and impotence and failure; he perversely prefers a spirituality that turns away from life toward death. Professor Trilling explains his perversity as a refusal "to admit and consent to the *conditioned* nature of man," to bow his neck to modern rationality: "If pleasure is indeed the principle of his being, he is as *known* as the sum of 2 and 2; he is a mere object of reason, of that rationality of the Revolution which is established upon the primacy of the principle of pleasure ("The Fate of Pleasure").

Now of course human life is lived under and through all kinds of conditions; we are not absolutely free, insouciant spirits. The Underground Man would really be crazy if he refused to admit or consent to this. But what drives him nearly crazy is the possibility that we are *nothing but* the product of conditions. His perversity and unreasonableness consist in refusing to accept what he cannot refute: the reasoning of scientific determinism, what he calls "the laws of nature." The painful issue for him is not the conditioned nature of man, but the *absolutely* conditioned nature of man, the scientific arguments for which *he cannot refute*. At one point in his argument Professor Trilling applies the Freudian term "drive" to the pleasure principle—the Underground Man fights against being "driven" absolutely. In his ravings, it is true, he sometimes seems to be lashing out against all conditions. But that is because Dostoevsky is portraying a frightened living person and not just an argument; *Notes from the Underground* is after all a story. Helpless to refute the rationality of the "Crystal Palace" and the "nineteenth century" and hang onto his freedom, he falls back like a child on mere defiance and perversity, the only freedom left him: "Of course I cannot break through the wall [of deterministic law] by battering my head against it if I really have not the strength to knock it down, but I am not going to be reconciled to it simply because it is a stone wall and I have not the strength." An ignorant, contrary child and also a spiteful devil, he is the modern poet-hero, a notorious adolescent who refuses to accept reality—the exiguous reality of a scientism which "excludes value from the essence of matter of fact" (to quote Whitehead again) and exiles the human freedom to choose the good into the unreal realm of modern spirit (*Science and the Modern World*).

The Underground Man rejects not pleasure in principle, but the pleasure principle, the *Lustprinzip*, because it operates with automatic compulsion, uncontrolled by any idea of what is good. He is a modern poet, which is to say a poet-philosopher; he rejects *modern* pleasure, which is poisoned for him by its inability to justify itself except on grounds of brute necessity, on the grounds that it is necessarily what it is; and by its *indifference* to the question of justifying itself. He does not, with perverted pride, choose unpleasure, as Professor Trilling has it; his plight is that he does not know what pleasure, *true* pleasure, is anymore (*Science and the Modern World*). He does not know. And because he does not know, he is powerless to act like a man — for how should a man act? — falling into a void of unlife. But in facing this he is a man.

In Gregor Samsa there is no trace of pride or vanity about himself as a superior suffering spiritual being. The Kafka artist-hero is a genuine hunger artist who fasts because he must, because the diet of the world cannot satisfy his spiritual hunger, and not because he has made hunger into the supreme good. "Forgive me, everybody," the Hunger Artist whispers in the story of that name when he is dying in his cage. "Of course we forgive you," replies the circus overseer.

> "I always wanted you to admire my fasting," said the hunger artist. "We do admire it," said the overseer, affably. "But you shouldn't admire it," said the hunger artist. "Well then we don't admire it," said the overseer, "but why shouldn't we admire it?" "Because I have to fast, I can't help it," said the hunger artist. "What a fellow you are," said the overseer, "and why can't you help it?" "Because," said the hunger artist, lifting his head a little and speaking, with his lips pursed, as if for a kiss, right into the overseer's ear, so that no syllable might be lost, "because I couldn't find the food I liked. If I had found it, believe me, I should have made no fuss and eaten my fill like you or anyone else."

Metamorphosis of the Metaphor

Stanley Corngold

To judge from its critical reception, Franz Kafka's *The Metamorphosis (Die Verwandlung)* is the most haunting and universal of all his stories; and yet Kafka never claimed for it any particular distinction. His comments on the story in his letters and diaries are almost entirely negative. "A pity," he wrote to Felice Bauer on December 6, 1912, "that in many passages in the story my states of exhaustion and other interruptions and worries about other things are clearly inscribed. It could certainly have been more cleanly done; you see that from the sweet pages." His disappointment with the ending was especially great. "My little story is finished, but today's conclusion doesn't make me happy at all; it should have been better, no doubt about it." This charge recurs in the diary entry for January 19, 1914: "Great antipathy to 'Metamorphosis.' Unreadable ending. Imperfect almost to its very marrow. It would have turned out much better if I had not been interrupted at the time by the business trip."

Kafka's own sense of *The Metamorphosis* tends, I think, to shift the weight of its significance towards its beginning. This result is confirmed by other evidence establishing what might be termed the general and fundamental priority of the beginning in Kafka's works. One thinks of the innumerable openings to stories which are scattered throughout the diaries and notebooks, which are suddenly born and as swiftly vanish, leaving undeveloped the endless dialectical structures they contain. Kafka explicitly expressed, on October 16, 1921, "The misery of a perpetual beginning, the lack of the illusion that anything is more than a beginning or even as much as a beginning." For

From *Mosaic* 3, no. 4 (1970). © 1970 by the University of Manitoba Press.

Dieter Hasselblatt "[Kafka's prose] is a fugitive from the beginning, it does not strive towards the end: *initiofugal*, not final. And since it takes the impulse of its progression from what is set forth or what is lying there at the outset, it cannot be completed. The end, the conclusion, is unimportant next to the opening situation."

One is directed, it would seem, by these empirical and theoretical considerations, to formulate the overwhelming question of *The Metamorphosis* as the question of the meaning of its beginning. What fundamental intention inspires the opening sentence of *The Metamorphosis*: "When Gregor Samsa woke up one morning from unsettling dreams, he found himself changed in his bed into a monstrous vermin (*ungeheures Ungeziefer*)". (All translations of *The Metamorphosis* are from *The Metamorphosis*, newly translated and edited by Stanley Corngold.) In answering this question we shall do well to keep in mind, in the words of a recent critic, "the identity [of the beginning] as *radical* starting point: the intransitive and conceptual aspect, that which has no object but its own constant clarification" (Edward Said, "Beginnings," *Salmagundi* [Fall 1968]). Much of the action of *The Metamorphosis* consists of Kafka's attempt to come to terms with its beginning.

The opening of *The Metamorphosis* recounts the metamorphosis of a man into a monstrous, verminous bug, but in doing this it appears to accomplish still another metamorphosis: it metamorphoses a common figure of speech. This second metamorphosis emerges in the light of the hypothesis proposed, in 1947, by Günther Anders: "Kafka's sole point of departure is . . . *ordinary language*. . . . More precisely: *he draws from the resources on hand, the figurative character (Bildcharakter), of language. He takes metaphors at their word (beim Wort). For example*: Because Gregor Samsa wants to live as an artist (i.e., as a '*Luftmensch*' — one who lives on air, lofty and free-floating), in the eyes of the highly respectable, hard-working world he is a 'nasty bug' ('*dreckiger Käfer*'): and so in *The Metamorphosis* he wakes up as a beetle whose idea of happiness is to be sticking to the ceiling" (*Kafka — Pro and Contra*). For Günther Anders *The Metamorphosis* originates in the transformation of a familiar metaphor into a fictional being literally existing as this metaphor. The story develops, as aspects of the metaphor are enacted in minute detail.

Anders's evidence for this view is furnished partly by his entire comprehension of Kafka: "What Kafka describes are . . . existing things, the world, as it appears to the stranger (namely strange)." Anders adduces, moreover, examples of everyday figures of speech which, taken literally, inspire stories and scenes in Kafka. "Language says 'To feel it with your own body' ('*Am eignen Leibe etwas erfahren*') when it wants to express the reality of experience. This is the basis of Kafka's '*In the Penal Colony*,' in which the criminal's punishment is not communicated to him by word of mouth, but is instead scratched into his body with a needle."

Anders's hypothesis has been taken up in Walter Sokel's writings on *The Metamorphosis*. The notion of the "extended metaphor," which Sokel considers in an early essay to be "significant" and "interesting" though "insufficient as a total explanation of *Metamorphosis*," reemerges in *The Writer in Extremis* as a crucial determinant of Expressionism: "The character Gregor Samsa has been transformed into a metaphor that states his essential self, and this metaphor in turn is treated like an actual fact. Samsa does not call himself a cockroach; instead he wakes up to find himself one." Expressionist prose, for Sokel, is to be defined precisely by such "extended metaphors, metaphoric visualizations of emotional situations, uprooted from any explanatory context." In *Franz Kafka — Tragik and Ironie*, the factual character of the Kafkan metaphor is reasserted: "In Kafka's work, as in the dream, symbol is fact. . . . A world of pure significance, of naked expression, is represented deceptively as a sequence of empirical facts." But in *Franz Kafka*, Sokel first states the "pure significance" of Kafka's literalization of the metaphor:

> German usage applies the term *Ungeziefer* (vermin) to persons considered low and contemptible, even as our usage of "cockroach" describes a person deemed a spineless and miserable character. The traveling salesman Gregor Samsa, in Kafka's *The Metamorphosis*, is "like a cockroach" because of his spineless and abject behavior and parasitic wishes. However, Kafka drops the word "like" and has the metaphor become reality when Gregor Samsa wakes up finding himself turned into a giant vermin. With this metamorphosis, Kafka reverses the original act of metamorphosis carried out by thought when it forms metaphor; for metaphor is always "metamorphosis." Kafka transforms metaphor back into his fictional reality, and this counter-metamorphosis becomes the starting point of his tale.

The sequence of Sokel's reflections on Anders's hypothesis contains an important shift of emphasis. Initially the force of *The Metamorphosis* is felt to lie in the choice and "extension" (dramatization) of the powerful metaphor. To confirm his view, Sokel cites Johannes Urzidil's recollection of a conversation with Kafka: "Once Kafka said to me: 'To be a poet means to be strong in metaphors. The greatest poets were always the most metaphorical ones. They were those who recognized the deep mutual concern, yes, even the identity of things between which nobody noticed the slightest connection before. It is the range and the scope of the metaphor which makes one a poet'" (John (*sic*) Urzidil, "Recollections," *The Kafka Problem*, ed. Angel Flores). But in his later work, Sokel locates the origin of Kafka's "poetry," not in the metamorphosis of reality accomplished by the metaphor, but in the "counter-metamorphosis" accomplished by the transformation of the metaphor. Kafka's "taking over" images from ordinary speech enacts a second metaphorization (*metaphero* = carry over) — one that concludes in the literalization and hence the metamorphosis of the metaphor. This point once made, the genuine importance of Kafka's remarks to Urzidil can be revealed through their irony. In describing the poet as one "strong in metaphors," Kafka is describing writers other than himself; for he is the writer, par excellence, who came to detect in metaphorical language a crucial obstacle to his own enterprise.

Kafka's critique of the metaphor begins early, in the phantasmagoric story "Description of a Struggle" (1904–1905). The first-person narrator addresses with exaggerated severity another persona of the author:

> "Now I realize, by God, that I guessed from the very beginning the state you are in. Isn't it something like a fever, a seasickness on land, a kind of leprosy? Don't you feel it's this very feverishness which is preventing you from being properly satisfied with the genuine (*wahrhaftigen*) names of things, and that now, in your frantic haste, you're just pelting them with any old (*zufällige*) names? You can't do it fast enough. But hardly have you run away from them when you've forgotten the names you gave them. The poplar in the fields, which you've called the 'Tower of Babel' because you didn't want to know it was a poplar, sways again without a name, so you have to call it 'Noah in his cups.' "

In the sense that "language is fundamentally metaphoric," in the sense that naming links the significations within words (*Sprachinhalte*) to the "significations to which words accrue," [as Derrida, Weisgerber, and Heidegger argue] this critique of naming amounts to a critique of the metaphor. But what is remarkable about this passage is its dissatisfaction with both ordinary names and figurative names. With the irony of exaggerated emphasis, it calls the conventional link of name and thing "genuine" and the act of renaming things, an act which generates metaphors, arbitrary. The new metaphor leaves no permanent trace; it is the contingent product of a fever, or worse: it arises from deliberate bad faith, the refusal to accept the conventional bond of word and thing. The exact status of ordinary names remains unclear; but what is important is that Kafka sees no advance in replacing them with the figures of poetic language.

In a diary entry for December 27, 1911, Kafka states his despair of a particular attempt at metaphor: "An incoherent assumption is thrust like a board between the actual feeling and the metaphor of the description." Kafka has begun this diary entry confidently, claiming to have found an image analogous to a moral sentiment: "This feeling of falsity that I have while writing might be represented in the following image." The image Kafka constructs is of a man in front of two holes in the ground, one to the right and one to the left; he is waiting for something that can rise up only out of the hole to the right. Instead of this, appearances rise up, one after the other, from the left; they try to attract his attention and succeed finally in covering up even the hole on his right. At this stage of the construction, the image predominates in its materiality. As the image is developed, however, the role of the spectator is developed, who expels these appearances upwards and in all directions in the hope "that after the false appearances have been exhausted, the true will finally appear." But precisely at the point of conjuring up "truthful apparitions," the metaphorist feels most critically the inadequacy of this figurative language: "How weak this image is." And he concludes with the complaint that between his sentiment and figurative language there is no true coherence (though he cannot, ironically, say this without having recourse to a figure of speech). Now what is crucial here is that an image which is mainly material has failed to represent the sentiment of writing; and though it has been replaced by one which introduces the consciousness of an observer, between the moral sentiment of writing and an act of perception there is no true connection either. If the writer finds it difficult to construct metaphors for "a feeling of falsity," how much graver must be his difficulty in constructing figures for genuine feelings, figures for gratifying the desire "to write all my anxiety entirely out of me, write it into the depths of the paper just as it comes out of the depths of me, or write it in such a way that I could draw what I had written into me completely"?

Kafka's awareness of the limitations of figurative language continues to grow more radical. The desire to represent a state-of-mind immediately in language, in a form consubstantial with that consciousness, and hence to create symbols, cannot be gratified through figurative language. "For everything outside the phenomenal world, language can only be used in the manner of an allusion (*andeutungsweise*), but never even approximately in the manner of a simile (*vergleichsweise*), since corresponding as it does to the phenomenal world, it is concerned only with property and its relations" (*Dearest Father*, translated by Ernst Kaiser and Eithne Wilkins). But try as language will to reduce itself to its allusive function, it continues to find itself dependent on the metaphor, on accomplishing states-of-mind by means of material analogues.

Kafka writes on December 6, 1921: "Metaphors are one among many things which make me despair of writing. Writing's lack of independence of the world, its dependence on the maid who tends the fire, on the cat warming itself by the stove; it is even dependent on the poor old human being warming himself by the stove. All these are independent activities ruled by their own laws; only writing is helpless, cannot live in itself, is a joke and a despair." Indeed, the question arises, what truth could even a language determinedly nonfigurative — in Kafka's word, "allusive" — possess? The parable employs language allusively, but in the powerful fable, "On Parables," Kafka writes: "All these parables really set out to say merely that the incomprehensible is incomprehensible, and we know that already." At this point, it is clear, the literary enterprise is seen in its radical problematicalness. The growing desperation of Kafka's critique of metaphorical language leads to the result (in the words of Maurice Blanchot) that, at the end of Kafka's life, "the exigency of the truth of this other world [of sheer inwardness desiring salvation] henceforth surpasses in his eyes the exigency of the work of art" ("The Diaries: The Exigency of the Work of Art," translated by Lyall H. Powers, *Franz Kafka Today*, edited by Angel Flores and Homer Swander). This situation does not suggest the renunciation of writing, but only the clearest possible perception of its limitations, a perception which emerges through Kafka's perplexity before, and despair of escaping, the metaphor in the work of art.

Kafka's "counter-metamorphosis" of the metaphor in *The Metamorphosis* is inspired by his fundamental objection to the metaphor. This is accomplished — so Anders and Sokel propose — through the literalization of the metaphor. But is this true? What does it mean, exactly, to literalize a metaphor?

The metaphor designates something (A) *as* something (B), something in the quality of something not itself. To say that someone is a verminous bug is to designate a moral sensibility as something unlike itself, as a material sensation complicated, of course, by the atmosphere of horror which this sensation evokes. We shall call, with I. A. Richards, the *tenor* of the metaphor, (A), the thing designated, occulted, replaced, but otherwise established by the context of the figure; and the *vehicle*, the metaphor proper, (B), that thing *as* which the tenor is designated (*The Philosophy of Rhetoric*). If the metaphor is taken out of its context, however, if it is taken literally, it no longer functions as a vehicle but as a name, directing us to (B) as an abstraction or an object in the world. Moreover, it directs us to (B) in the totality of its qualities, and not, as the vehicle, to only those qualities of (B) which can be assigned to (A).

This analysis will suggest, I think, the paradoxical consequence of "taking the metaphor literally," supposing now that such a thing is possible. Reading the figure literally, we go to (B), an object in the world in its totality, yet, reading it metaphorically, we go to (B) only in its quality as a predicate of (A). The object (B) is quite plainly unstable and, hence, so is (A); as literalization proceeds, as we attempt to experience in (B) more and more qualities that can be accommodated by (A), *we metamorphose (A)*; but we must stop before the metamorphosis is complete, if the metaphor is to be preserved and (A) is to remain unlike (B). If, now, the tenor, as in *The Metamorphosis*, is a human consciousness, the increasing literalization of the vehicle transforms the tenor into a monster.

This genesis of monsters occurs independently of the nature of the vehicle. The intent towards literalization of a metaphor linking a human consciousness and a material sensation produces a monster in every instance, no matter whether the vehicle is odious or not, no matter whether we begin with the metaphor of a "louse" or of the man who is a rock or sterling. But it now appears that Anders is not correct to suggest that in *The Metamorphosis* literalization of the metaphor is actually accomplished; for then we should have not an indefinite monster but simply a bug. Indeed the progressive deterioration of Gregor's body suggests ongoing metamorphosis, the *process* of literalization and not its end-state. And Sokel's earlier formulation would not appear to be tenable: the metaphor is not treated "like an actual fact." Only the alien cleaning woman gives Gregor Samsa the factual, the entomological identity of the "dung beetle"; but precisely "to forms of address like these Gregor would not respond." The cleaning woman does not know that a metamorphosis has occurred, that in this insect shape there is a human consciousness, one superior at times to the ordinary consciousness of Gregor Samsa. Our analysis shows that the metamorphosis in the Samsa household of a man into a vermin is unsettling not only because a vermin is unsettling, and not only because the vivid representation of a "human louse" is unsettling, but because the indeterminate, fluid crossing of a human tenor and a material vehicle is in itself unsettling. Gregor is at one moment pure rapture, at another, very nearly pure dung beetle, at times grossly human, at times airily buglike. In shifting incessantly the relation of Gregor's mind and body, Kafka shatters the suppositious unity of ideal tenor and bodily vehicle within the metaphor. This destruction must distress common sense, which defines itself by such "genuine" relations, such natural assertions of analogues between consciousness and matter, and this way masks the knowledge of its own strangeness. The ontological legitimation for asserting analogues is missing in Kafka, who maintains the most ruthless division between the fire of the spirit and the principle of the world: "What we call the world of the senses is the Evil in the spiritual world" (*Dearest Father*).

The distortion of the metaphor in *The Metamorphosis* is inspired by a radical aesthetic intention, which proceeds by destruction and results in creation — of a monster, virtually nameless, existing as an opaque sign. "The name alone, revealed through a natural death, not the living soul, vouches for that in man which is immortal" (Adorno). But what is remarkable in *The Metamorphosis* is that "the immortal part" of the writer accomplishes itself odiously, in the quality of an indeterminacy sheerly negative. The exact sense of his intention is captured in the "*Ungeziefer*," a word which cannot be expressed by the English words "bug" or "vermin." "*Ungeziefer*" derives (as Kafka probably knew) from the late Middle High German word originally meaning "the unclean animal not suited for sacrifice." If for Kafka "writing is a form of prayer" (*Dearest Father*), this act of writing reflects its own hopelessness. As a distortion of the "genuine" names of things, without significance as a metaphor or as literal fact, the monster of *The Metamorphosis* is, like writing itself, a "fever" and a "despair."

The metamorphosis of a vermin-metaphor cannot be understood as a real vermin, as that biting and blood-sucking creature to which, for example, Kafka has his father compare him in his *Letter to His Father*. But it may be illuminated by the link which Kafka established earlier between the bug and the activity of writing itself. In the story "Wedding Preparations in the Country" (1907), of which only a fragment survives, Kafka conjures a hero, Eduard Raban, reluctant to take action in the world (he is supposed to go to the country to arrange his wedding); Raban dreams instead of autonomy, self-sufficiency, and omnipotence. Kafka finds for this transparent reflection of his early literary consciousness the emblem of a beetle, about which there hovers an odd indeterminacy:

> "And besides, can't I do it the way I always used to as a child in matters that were dangerous? I don't even need to go to the country myself, it isn't necessary. I'll send my clothed body. If it staggers out of the door of my room, the staggering will indicate not fear but its nothingness. Nor is it a sign of excitement if it stumbles on the stairs, if it travels into the country, sobbing as it goes, and there eats its supper in tears. For I myself am meanwhile lying in my bed, smoothly covered over with the yellow-brown blanket, exposed to the breeze that is wafted through that seldom aired room. The carriages and people in the street

move and walk hesitantly on shining ground, for I am still dreaming. Coachmen and pedestrians are shy, and every step they want to advance they ask as a favor from me, by looking at me. I encourage them and they encounter no obstacle.

"As I lie in bed I assume the shape of a big beetle, a stag beetle or a cockchafer, I think. . . .

"The form of a large beetle, yes. Then I would pretend it was a matter of hibernating, and I would press my little legs to my bulging belly. And I would whisper a few words, instructions to my sad body, which stands close beside me, bent. Soon I shall have done—it bows, it goes swiftly, and it will manage everything efficiently while I rest."

The figure of the omnipotent bug is positive throughout this passage and suggests the inwardness of the act of writing rendered in its power and freedom, in its mystic exaltation, evidence of which abounds in Kafka's earliest diaries:

The special nature of my inspiration . . . is such that I can do everything, and not only what is directed to a definite piece of work. When I arbitrarily write a single sentence, for instance, "He looked out of the window," it already has perfection.

My happiness, my abilities, and every possibility of being useful in any way have always been in the literary field. And here I have, to be sure, experienced states . . . in which I completely dwelt in every idea, but also filled every idea, and in which I not only felt myself at my boundary, but at the boundary of the human in general.

How everything can be said, how for everything, for the strangest fancies, there waits a great fire in which they perish and rise up again.

But this is only one side of Kafka's poetic consciousness. The other is expressed through the narrator's hesitation in defining his trance by means of an objective correlative ("a stag beetle . . . , I think"), which suggests, beyond his particular distress, the general impossibility of the metaphor's naming immediately with a material image the being of an inward state, and hence a doubt that will go to the root of writing itself. After 1912 there will be few such positive emblems for the inwardness and solitude of the act of writing; this "beautiful" bug (Sokel, *Franz Kafka — Tragik und Ironie*) is projected in ignorance; the truer emblem of the alien poetic consciousness, which "has no basis, no stability" (*Briefe 1902–1924*), which must suffer "the eternal torments of dying," becomes the vermin Gregor. The movement from the beautiful bug Raban to the monstrous bug Gregor marks an accession of self-knowledge — an increasing awareness of the poverty and shortcomings of writing.

The direction of Kafka's reflection on literature is fundamentally defined, however, by "The Judgment," the story written immediately before *The Metamorphosis.* "The Judgment" struck Kafka as a breakthrough into his own style; after the night he spent composing it, Kafka wrote in his diary, with a fine elation, "Only *in this way* can writing be done, only with such coherence, with such a complete opening out of the body and the soul." But in his later interpretation of the story, Kafka described it in a somewhat more sinister tonality, as having "come out of me like a regular birth, covered with filth and mucus." The image has the violence and inevitability of a natural process, but its filth and mucus cannot fail to remind the reader of the strange birth which is the subject of Kafka's next story — the incubus trailing filth and mucus through the household of its family.

Mainly two aspects of "The Judgment," I think, inspire in Kafka a sense of its authenticity important enough to be commemorated in the figure of the vermin. First, the figure of the friend in Russia represents with the greatest clarity to date the negativity of this "business" of writing (the friend is said by the father to be "yellow enough to be thrown away"; secondly, "The Judgment," like *The Metamorphosis*, develops, as the implications of a distorted metaphor are enacted: "The Judgment" metamorphoses the father's "judg-ment" or "estimate" into a fatal "verdict," a death-"sentence."

Kafka's awareness that "The Judgment" originates from the distortion of the metaphor dictates the conclusion of his "interpretation." The highly formal tonality of this structural analysis surprises the reader, following as it does on the organic simile of the sudden birth: "The friend is the link between father and son, he is their strongest common bond. Sitting alone at his window, Georg rummages voluptuously in this consciousness of what they have in common, believes he has his father within him, and would be at peace with everything if it were not for a fleeting, sad thoughtfulness. In the course of the story the father . . . uses the common bond of the friend to set himself up as Georg's antagonist." This analysis employs the structural model of the metamorphosed metaphor. At first Georg considers the father *as* the friend; his friend, as the metaphor of the father. But Georg's doom is to take the metaphor literally, to suppose that by himself sharing the quality of the friend, he possesses the father in fact. Now in a violent counter-movement the father distorts the initial metaphor, drawing the friend's existence into himself; and Georg, who now feels "what they have in common . . . only as something foreign, something that has become independent, that he has never given enough protection," accepts his sentence.

It is this new art, generated from the distortion of relations modelled on the metaphor, which came to Kafka as an elation, a gross new birth, and a sentence; the aesthetic intention comes to light negatively when it must express itself through so tormented and elliptical a strategem as the metamorphosis of the metaphor. The restrictedness and misery of this art is the explicit subject of *The Metamorphosis*; the invention which henceforth shapes Kafka's existence as a writer is original, arbitrary and fundamentally strange. In a later autobiographical note he writes: "Everything he does seems to him extraordinarily new, it is true, but also, consistent with this incredible abundance of new things, extraordinarily amateurish, indeed scarcely tolerable, incapable of becoming history, breaking the chain of the generations, cutting off for the first time at its most profound source the music of the world, which before him could at least be divined. Sometimes in his arrogance he is more afraid for the world than for himself" (*The Great Wall of China*). Kafka's pride in his separateness is just equal to his nostalgia for "the music of the world." We shall think of the violently distorted metaphor which yields this figure, of Gregor Samsa, who in responding to his sister's violin playing, causes this music to be broken off. That being who lives as a distortion of nature; who, without a history and without a future, still maintains a certain sovereignty; conjures through the extremity of his separation the clearest possible idea of the music he cannot possess.

In his letter of July 5, 1922, to Max Brod, Kafka envisions the writer as inhabiting a place outside the house of life—as a dead man, as one among the "departed," of the *Reflections*, who long to be flooded back to us. It cannot be otherwise; the writer has no genuine existence ("[*ist*] *etwas nicht Bestehendes*"); what he produces is devilish, "the reward for devil's duty—this descent to the dark forces, this unbinding of spirits by nature bound, dubious embraces and whatever else may go on below, of which one no longer knows anything above ground when in the sunlight one writes stories. Perhaps there is also another kind of writing. I only know this kind." "Yet," as Erich Heller remarks, "it remains dubious who this 'one' is who 'writes stories in the sunlight.' Kafka himself? 'The Judgment'—and sunlight? 'The Metamorphosis' . . . and sunlight . . . ? How must it have been 'below ground' if 'above ground' blossoms like these were put forth?" (*Briefe an Felice*, edited by Erich Heller and Jürgen Born).

Kafka's art, which Kafka elsewhere calls a conjuration of spirits, brings into the light of language the experience of descent and doubt. And even this experience has to be repeated perpetually: "Thus I waver, continually fly to the summit of the mountain, but then fall back in a moment. . . . [It] is not death, alas, but the eternal torments of dying." There is no true duration in this desperate flight; conjuring his own death, Kafka writes: "The writer in me of course will die at once, for such a figure has no basis, has no substance, isn't even of dust; is only a construction of the craving for enjoyment. This is the writer." The self-indulgence which defines the writer is that of the being who perpetually reflects on himself and others. The word "figure," in the passage above, can be taken à la lettre: the writer is defined by his verbal figures, conceived at a distance from life, inspired by a devilish aesthetic detachment craving to indulge itself; but he suffers, too, the meaninglessness of the figure uprooted from the language of life—the dead figure. Kafka's spirit then does spend itself "zur Illuminierung meines Leichnams," in lighting up—but also in furnishing figural decorations for—his corpse.

It is this dwelling outside the house of life, "Schriftstellersein," the negative condition of writing as such, which is named in The Metamorphosis; but it cannot name itself directly, in a language that designates things that are, or in the figures that suggest the relations between things constituting the common imagination of life. Instead Kafka utters in The Metamorphosis a word for a being unacceptable to man (ungeheuer) and unacceptable to God (Ungeziefer), a word unsuited either to intimate speech or to prayer. This word evokes a distortion without visual identity or self-awareness—engenders, for a hero, a pure sign. The creature of The Metamorphosis is not a self speaking or being silent but language itself (parole)—a word broken loose from the context of language (language), fallen into a void the meaning of which it cannot signify, near others who cannot understand it.

As the story of a metamorphosed metaphor, The Metamorphosis is not just one among Kafka's stories but an exemplarily Kafkan story; the title reflects the generative principle of Kafka's fiction—a metamorphosis of the function of language. In organizing itself around a distortion of ordinary language, The Metamorphosis projects into its center a sign which absorbs its own significance (as Gregor's opaque body occludes his awareness of self), and thus aims in an opposite direction from the art of the symbol; for there, in the words of Merleau-Ponty, the sign is "devoured" by its signification (Phénoménologie de la perception). The outcome of this tendency of The Metamorphosis is its ugliness. Symbolic art, modelled on the metaphor which occults the signifier to the level of signification, strikes us as beautiful: our notion of the beautiful harmony of sign and significance is one dominated by the human signification, by the form of the person which in Schiller's classical conception of art "extirpates the material reference." These expectations are disappointed by the opaque and impoverished sign in Kafka. His art devours the human meaning of itself, and indeed must soon raise the question of a suitable nourishment. It is thus strictly internally coherent that the vermin — the word without significance — should divine fresh nourishment and affinity in music, the language of signs without significance.

But the song which Gregor hears does not transform his suffering; the music breaks off; the monster finds nourishment in a cruder fantasy of anger and possession. This scene communicates the total discrepancy between the vermin's body and the cravings appropriate to it, and the other sort of nourishment for which he yearns; the moment produces, not symbolic harmony, but the intolerable tension of irreconcilables. In Kafka's unfathomable sentence: "Was he an animal, that music could move him so?", paradox echoes jarringly without end.

At the close of *The Metamorphosis* Gregor is issued a death-sentence by his family which he promptly takes over as his own; he then passes into a vacant trance.

> He had pains, of course, in his whole body, but it seemed to him as if they were gradually getting weaker and weaker and would finally go away entirely. The rotten apple in his back and the inflamed area around it, which were completely covered with fluffy dust, already hardly bothered him. He thought back on his family with deep emotion and love. His conviction that he would have to disappear was, if possible, even stronger than his sister's. In this state of empty and peaceful reflection, he remained until the tower clock struck three in the morning.

He is empty of all practical concerns; his body has dwindled to a mere dry husk, substantial enough to have become sonorous, too substantial not to have been betrayed by the promise of harmony in music. He suggests Christ, the Christ of John (19:30) but not of Matthew (27:50) or Mark (15:37), for Gregor's last moment is silent and painless. "He still sensed that outside the window everything was beginning to grow bright. Then, against his will, his head sank down to the floor, and from his nostrils came his last weak stream of breath." For a moment the dim desert of Gregor's world grows luminous; his opaque body, progressively impoverished, achieves a faint translucency. Through the destruction of the specious harmony of the metaphor and the aesthetic claims of the symbol, Kafka engenders another sort of beauty and, with this, closes a circle of reflection on his own work.

For, in 1910, just before his mature art originates as the distortion of the metaphor, Kafka wrote in the story fragment, " 'You,' I said . . .": "Already what protected me seemed to dissolve here in the city. I was beautiful in the early days, for this dissolution takes place as an apotheosis, in which everything that holds us to life flies away, but even in flying away illumines us for the last time with its human light" (*Diaries*).

At the close of *The Metamorphosis* the ongoing metamorphosis of the metaphor accomplishes itself through a consciousness empty of all practical attention and a body that preserves its opacity, but in so dwindled a form that it achieves the condition of a painless translucency, a kind of beauty. In creating in the vermin a figure for the distortion of the metaphor, the generative principle of his art, Kafka underscores the negativity of writing, but at the same time enters the music of the historical world at a crucial juncture; his art reveals at its root a powerful romantic aesthetic tradition associated with the names of Rousseau, Hölderlin, Wordsworth, Schlegel, Solger, which criticizes symbolic form and metaphorical diction in the name of a kind of allegorical language. The figures of this secular allegory do not refer doctrinally to Scripture but to the source of the decision to constitute them. They replace the dogmatic unity of sign and significance with the temporal relation of the sign to its luminous source. This relation comes to light through the temporal difference between the allegorical sign and the sign prefiguring it; the exact meaning of the signs is less important than the temporal character of their relation. The vermin that alludes to vermin-figures in Kafka's early work, whose death amid increasing luminousness alludes casually to Christ's, is just such a figure. But to stress now the temporal character of the metamorphosed metaphor of *The Metamorphosis* is to distinguish it fundamentally from the "extended metaphor" of Sokel's discussion; for in this organistic conception of the figure, sign and significance coincide as forms of extension. And if expressionism is to be defined by its further extension of metaphor, then *The Metamorphosis* cannot be accommodated in an expressionist tradition.

But though *The Metamorphosis* joins an allegorical tradition within romanticism, it does so only for a moment before departing radically from it. The light in which Gregor dies is said explicitly to emanate from outside the window and not from a source within the subject. The creature turned away from life, facing death, and as such a pure sign of the poetic consciousness, keeps for Kafka its opaque and tellurian character. It is as a distorted body that Gregor is struck by the light; and it is in this light principally unlike the source of poetic creation that the work of art just comes to recognize its own truth. For, wrote Kafka, "our art is a way of being dazzled by truth;

the light on the flinching, grimacing face (*zurückweichenden Fratzengesicht*) is true, and nothing else" (*Dearest Father*). Because the language of Kafka's fiction originates so knowingly from a reflection on ordinary speech, it cannot show the truth except as a solid body reflecting the light, a blank fragment of "what we call the world of the senses, [which] is the Evil in the spiritual world (*Dearest Father*).

And so the figure of the nameless vermin remains principally opaque. More fundamental than the moment of translucency; reflecting itself not so much in the dawn as in the fact that this moment is obtained only at death and without a witness; is the horror that writing could never amount to anything more than the twisted grimace on which glances a light not its own. Here the essentially linguistic imagination of Kafka joins him to a disruptive modern tradition, described in these words of Michel Foucault:

> The literature of our time is fascinated by the being of language. . . . As such, it brings sharply to light in their empirical vividness the fundamental forms of finitude. From inside language experienced and traversed as a language, in the play of its possibilities taken to their limit, what comes to light is that man is "finite"; and that arriving at the summit of all possible utterance, it is not to the heart of himself he comes, but to the edge of that which limits him: that region where death prowls, where thought fades out, where the promise of the origin retreats indefinitely. . . . And as if this probing of the forms of finitude in language could not be borne . . . it has manifested itself inside madness—the figure of finitude thus appearing in language as that which discloses itself in it but also before it, on its near side, as this shapeless, mute, meaningless region in which language can liberate itself. And it is truly in this space thus laid open that literature . . . more and more purely with Kafka, with Bataille, with Blanchot has appeared . . . as the experience of finitude.
>
> (*Words and Things*)

The Dramatic in Kafka's *Metamorphosis*

Evelyn Torton Beck

The fascination of *The Metamorphosis*, the most widely known and one of the most disturbing of Kafka's works, lies chiefly in the horror of its central metaphor — a man awakens one morning to find that he has become a giant bug — a situation which is presented with a matter-of-factness that is difficult to accept or comprehend. Begun in November and completed in December of 1912, only three months after the writing of "The Judgment," *The Metamorphosis* also reflects the direct impact of the Yiddish plays. Gordin's *The Savage One*, a classic of the Yiddish theater previously discussed [elsewhere] in connection with "The Judgment" and *Der Verschollene*, offered Kafka a model for making concrete the insect metaphor which he originally conceived in 1907. In the *Diaries* Kafka discusses *The Savage One* at length and outlines its plot in some detail:

> Parts of the plot of *Der Wilde Mensch* are very spirited. A young widow marries an old man with four children and immediately brings her lover, Vladimir Vorobeitchik, along into the marriage. The two proceed to ruin the whole family, Shmul Leiblich (Pipes) must soon hand over all his money and becomes sick, the oldest son, Simon (Klug), a student, leaves the house, Alexander becomes a gambler and drunkard, Lise (Tschissik) becomes a prostitute and Lemech (Löwy), the idiot, is driven to idiotic insanity by hate of Mrs. Selde, because she takes the place of his mother, and by love, because she is the first young woman to whom he feels close.

From *Kafka and the Yiddish Theater: Its Impact on His Work.* © 1971 by the Regents of the University of Wisconsin. University of Wisconsin Press, 1971.

> At this point the plot reaches a climax with the murder of Selde by Lemech.

Accurate though Kafka's synopsis is, it fails to emphasize the centrality of Lemekh, the "defective" son who becomes "the savage one" and whose situation (but for Gregor's physical disfigurement) closely parallels that of Gregor Samsa in *The Metamorphosis*. Like Lemekh, Gregor is barely tolerated in the home, and like him, is looked upon with disgust (particularly by the father) as an outcast whose very existence shames his family. In different ways, Gregor and Lemekh combine the same qualities of "thing" and "person." Both are presented as essentially simple, meek, self-effacing persons who become animal-like creatures because of a drastic transformation, which culminates in Gregor's death and Lemekh's murder of Zelde. Although Gregor's physical transformation is already completed when *The Metamorphosis* opens, while the change in Lemekh occurs more gradually, the process of progressive decay continues throughout both works. Thus, Gregor's metamorphosis parallels Lemekh's decline.

Each of the five characters in Kafka's story has a direct counterpart in Gordin's play. Besides Gregor and Lemekh, the two defective sons, there are the two fathers, Samsa Senior and Shmul Layblikh, who are "resurrected" (Samsa by his son's decline, Layblikh by his marriage); the two mother-figures, Mrs. Samsa and Zelde, who protect their sons and are adored by them; the two sisters, Grete and Liza, half-developed girls who eventually abandon the brothers to whom they are so closely attached; and the two housekeepers, who show no fear of the peculiar son and take charge of him.

The central metaphor of *The Metamorphosis* corresponds to the imagery which the housekeeper uses to describe Lemekh's position within his family: "They kill him if he comes in here, so he lies in his own room, days on end, with his eyes open, and stares, like an animal waiting to be sacrificed." ("Men harget im er zol nit aher nisht geyn, ligt er bay zikh, vi a hun in bney adam.") While Lemekh is said to stare at humans dumbly as if he were an animal, Gregor literally becomes an animal, and like Lemekh, is grateful to be allowed to look at and listen to his family from the darkness of his room: "He was sufficiently compensated for this worsening of his condition by the fact that towards evening the living-room door, which he used to watch intently for an hour or two beforehand, was always thrown open, so that lying in the darkness of his room, invisible to the family, he could see them all at the lamp-lit table and listen to their talk." ("So bekam er für diese Verschlimmerung seines Zustandes einen . . . Ersatz dadurch, dass immer gegen Abend die Wohnzimmertür, die er schon ein bis zwei Stunden vorher scharf zu beobachten pflegte, geöffnet wurde, so dass er, im Dunkel seines Zimmers liegend, vom Wohnzimmer aus unsichtbar, die ganze Familie beim beleuchteten Tische sehen und ihre Reden, . . . anhören durfte.") Whenever either Lemekh or Gregor tries to join his family, he is shooed into his designated quarters and beaten by an enraged father. Shmul Layblikh whips his son; Samsa uses a stick, a newspaper, and finally apples as weapons against Gregor. The two sons are described by similar epithets that set them apart from others, Lemekh as "the unsuccessful son" (*der nit gerutene zun*), Gregor as "the unfortunate son" (*der unglückliche Sohn*). Both epithets suggest misfortune, calamity, affliction, and conspicuous lack of success. The irrationality of Lemekh's behavior is paralleled by Gregor's confused responses to his changed physical condition. Gregor speaks of the morning's events as "foolishness," he feels "idiotic," he is described as "almost mad," "beside himself," and he believes that his solitary life "must have confounded his senses." ("Narrheiten"; "blödsinnig"; "fast wild geworden"; "ausser sich"; "seinen Verstand hatte verwirren müssen.")

The son's abnormal condition, which evokes parental fear and mistrust in both works, is at first interpreted (not only by the parents, but by the victim himself) as an illness that a doctor might cure. Layblikh shouts, "Woe, woe, help! help! . . . Quick, call people . . . , call a doctor . . . quick a doctor!" ("Vay mir, gevald, ratevet! ratevet! . . . Geshvind, ruft mentshn . . . , ruft a doctor . . . geshvind a doktor!") Similarly, Gregor's mother responds with "For God's sake, . . . perhaps he is terribly sick. . . . You must go for the doctor this very minute. Gregor is sick. Quick, get the doctor," and "Help, for God's sake, help!" ("Um Gottes willen, . . . er ist vielleicht schwerkrank. . . . Du musst augenblicklich zum Arzt. Gregor ist krank. Rasch um den Arzt." "Hilfe, um Gottes willen, Hilfe!") In each case, the son is suspected of deliberate malice. Lemekh is blamed for "making himself crazy"; Gregor is accused of stubbornness (*Starrsinn*) for not opening the door of his room. Later, Samsa senior fears that his son will commit "an act of violence" (*eine Gewalttat*), a suspicion shared by Shmul Layblikh, which becomes a fact in *The Savage One*. In story and play alike, the son's transformation manifests itself in loss of the ability to communicate. Gregor's voice is described as "a squeaking" (*ein Piepsen*), while Lemekh's speech takes on the quality of a weeping groan ("er krekhtst vaynend"); Gregor's words become completely incomprehensible, Lemekh's barely coherent. Both heroes suffer from their families' false assumption that because they cannot *be* understood, they necessarily cannot understand. For this reason, both are forced to listen to many unflattering, painful remarks carelessly made in their hearing.

The Oedipal conflict and the broader theme of incest, presented in highly exaggerated form in *The Savage One*, are also played upon in *The Metamorphosis*. In both works the son's love for the mother and sister becomes confused with sexual desire. Gregor's vision in which he imagines himself locked into his room with his sister, "protecting" her against all intruders, is clearly a sexual fantasy and parallels the scene in which Lemekh literally locks himself into a room with the sleeping Zelde and swears to keep her as his own. Gregor's rivalry with the father, made clear by the shifting of their economic roles, parallels Lemekh's open jealousy of Shmul. In both works the son faints or becomes dizzy whenever the father embraces his wife. In context, this blacking-out is symbolic of the son's inability to accept the union of his parents. Because Zelde is only Lemekh's stepmother and because she is, at the same time, a provocative young woman ill-matched to the decrepit old man she marries, Lemekh's jealousy can more easily be accounted for than Gregor's, at least on the literal level. Because Lemekh and Gregor are both sexually naive but physically adult, their sex drive expresses itself in ways which they can neither control nor comprehend. When Lemekh feels aroused by his new mother, he naively describes his feelings in rather obvious fire and heat imagery: "When you [Zelde] touch me I get hot"; "she touches me and I burn"; "a fire burns . . . I like it, it's good, let it burn." ("Az ir rirt mikh on vert mir heys"; "zi tsindet mikh on un ikh bren"; "es brent . . . es gefelt mir, es iz gut loz brenen.") A similar expression of intense physical desire, also phrased in terms of heat, is revealed by Gregor's uncontrollable urge to "save" his picture of the lady in furs: he "quickly crawled up to it and pressed himself against the glass, which held him fast and soothed his hot belly." ("[Er] kroch eilends hinauf und presste sich an das Glas, das ihn festhielt und seinem heissen Bauch wohltat.") Politzer correctly interprets Gregor's act as vicarious possession of the woman in the picture, a parallel to Lemekh's symbolic possession of Zelde, which occurs when he stabs her, repeating the words, "I have married . . . she is mine, my bride." ("Ikh hob khasene gehat . . . zi iz mayne, mayn kale.")

But suppressed sexuality is only one among the many thematic and technical devices tying Kafka's story to Gordin's play. Gregor's difficulties in getting out of bed produce in him a fantasy that is very close to the literal events portrayed in *The Savage One.* As he struggles, he imagines: "How simple it would be if he could get help. Two strong people—he thought of his father and the servant girl—would be amply sufficient; they would only have to thrust their arms under his convex back." ("Wie einfach alles wäre, wenn man ihm zu Hilfe käme. Zwei starke Leute—er dachte an seinen Vater und das Dienstmädchen—hätten vollständig genügt; sie hätten ihre Arme nur unter seinen gewölbten Rücken schieben . . . müssen.") In Gordin's play, when Lemekh falls into a faint he is literally rescued by two such helpers, his brother and the housekeeper. Lemekh's confused behavior, associated with his loss of rational control—"he crawls on the floor" (*er krikht oyf der erd*)—provides a direct, visual statement of the extent of his degradation. This is paralleled in *The Metamorphosis* by Gregor's crawling, which signals his acceptance of his animal condition, particularly in the second section, where it is not only a means of locomotion, but a diversion as well. In another comparison, Lemekh's hiding behind the drapes when he hears Zelde's footsteps is paralleled by Gregor's hiding under the couch beneath a draped sheet whenever his mother or sister enters the room.

Fainting as a theatrical device recurs in both *The Savage One* and in *The Metamorphosis*. In both works it serves to heighten the intensity of the action and to reveal strong emotion by direct, visual means. The staged quality of the scenes in which Gregor confronts his family—for example, the mother's melodramatic response to Gregor ("That made his mother scream again, she fled from the table and fell into the arms of his father, who hastened to catch her") ("Darüber schrie die Mutter neuerdings auf, flüchtete vom Tisch und fiel dem ihr entgegeneilenden Vater in die Arme") and her knocking over a pot of coffee as she flees from her son—creates a comic effect within the tragic circumstances that recalls the fusion of the tragic with the comic in the plays of the Yiddish theater.

Setting functions symbolically in both works. Lemekh expresses his feelings of isolation by reference to the furnishings of the newly redecorated family room, from which he is barred: "When there were not such [fancy] chairs and couches here, it used to be warm and friendly; now it is cold, gloomy, dark, sad, just as it is in here. (*Points to his heart.*)" ("Ven do iz nit geven azelkhe shtuln un divanen, iz do geven varm un fraylakh, haynt iz do kalt, pust, finster, troyrig, azoy vi bey mir ot a do. (*Tsaygt oyf zayn harts.*)" The condition of Gregor's room, filled with dirt, garbage, and cast-off furniture, perfectly reflects the family's disgust for their son and makes concrete Gregor's own feelings about himself by means a dramatist might employ. Lemekh's appraisal of his family's attitude—"For me and for you it would be better if I died. . . . Who wants me to live?" ("Far mir un far aykh volt beser geven az ikh zol shtarbn. . . . Ver vil ikh zol lebn?")—parallels Gregor's evaluation of his position: "The decision that he must disappear was one that he held to even more strongly than his sister, if that were possible." ("Seine Meinung darüber, dass er verschwinden müsse, war womöglich noch entschiedener als die seiner Schwester.")

Other symbols, central to story and play, further link *The Metamorphosis* to *The Savage One*. The image of the hospital is associated with the "illness" of the hero in both works. The bleak view of the gray hospital building which greets Gregor's vision as he awakens each morning is analogous to the institution in which Lemekh is eventually confined. The restraining power of the "iron jacket" into which Lemekh is locked parallel's Gregor's "armour-plated hard back," which literally imprisons him and is also symbolic of his spiritual limitations. ("Er lag auf seinem panzerartig harten Rücken.") Such symbolic details as response to music and loss of appetite are associated with the son's condition in both works. Lemekh remarks that music helps him to forget that he is not a person like others: when he hears music he forgets the whip and the beatings and thinks that he is only as much of an idiot as all others are. ("Zingt nokh, nokh, az men zingt ferges ikh az ikh bin nit aza mentsh vi ale yuden, ikh ferges in'm moment kantshik, un Shifras petsh un ikh mayn az ikh bin aza idyot vi ale mentshn.") The pathos of Lemekh's humor is paralleled by the grim irony of Gregor's rhetorical question "Was he an animal that music moved him so?" ("War er ein Tier, da ihn Musik so ergriff?") (Throughout the narrative Kafka makes use of dramatic irony based on Gregor's failure to comprehend fully the seriousness of his situation. For example, when he falls to the floor and suddenly feels physically comfortable for the first time since he awoke, he readily believes that "final relief from all his sufferings was directly at hand." ("Und schon glaubte er, die endgültige Besserung alles Leidens stehe unmittelbar bevor.") As events prove, he could hardly have been more mistaken.)

In handling setting in *The Metamorphosis* Kafka again adapts the techniques of the stage. Each section of the story is limited to a small, clearly defined area (Gregor's room and the living room); props are placed and accounted for as if they were to be made concrete on a stage. With the exception of Gregor, the characters are minimally developed and resemble the type characters of the drama, who fulfill one function or embody only a single trait. The movements of the characters are recorded with the precision of stage directions, and the exaggerated action often culminates in a grouping of characters that recalls the tableaux of the Yiddish theater. For example: "Now they were all watching him in melancholy silence. His mother lay in her chair, her legs stiffly outstretched and pressed together, her eyes almost closing for sheer weariness; his father and his sister were sitting beside each other, his sister's arm around the [father's] neck." ("Nun sahen ihn alle schweigend und traurig an. Die Mutter lag, die Beine ausgestreckt und aneinandergedrückt, in ihrem Sessel, die Augen fielen ihr vor Ermattung fast zu; der Vater und die Schwester sassen nebeneinander, die Schwester hatte ihre Hand um des Vaters Hals gelegt.")

Structurally, *The Metamorphosis* progresses like a drama, building through a series of crises (Gregor's three confrontations with the outside world) to a final denouement (Gregor's death and removal). The three chapters which make up *The Metamorphosis* correspond to the stages of Gregor's decline and relate to each other like the separate, self-contained acts of a play.

In content and function, the sentimental ending of *The Metamorphosis* exactly parallels the epilogue of *The Savage One* (with the important distinction that in *The Metamorphosis* Gregor dies, while in *The Savage One* Lemekh is reconciled with his family). At the end, both families vow to forget the events of the past and to look to the promise of the future, which is symbolized for both by the prospective marriage of the young daughter. Like the epilogue of *The Savage One*, the ending of *The Metamorphosis* not only seems contrived and false, but ironically, its realistic action seems far less convincing than the truly fantastic events of the body of the story. One is tempted to discount the aesthetically unsatisfying endings of both works.

A comparison of the role of the family in *The Metamorphosis* and *The Savage One* reveals that to a great degree the Samsas and the Layblikhs are similarly to blame for their sons' declines. Lemekh's all-consuming passion for his new stepmother is, at least in part, brought on by Zelde's carelessness in handling him, and is further aggravated by the father's total lack of compassion for his son. From the details that come to light in *The Metamorphosis*, it becomes clear that Gregor has not been treated fairly, that his family has shown him little compassion, and that in addition they have seriously exploited his willingness to be their sole support.

Although one would never assert that the metamorphosis can be fully explained as a metaphor for Gregor's subservience within the family or on the job, nevertheless, in order for the narrative to cohere, one must assume that Gregor's animal shape embodies some essential aspect of his previous human experience. Kafka deliberately leaves the meaning of his central symbol partially obscure; Gordin, however, provides us with an explicit key to his work, which aids our understanding of the Kafka story as well. Near the end of the play Lemekh's brother explains: "What—where is this savage one? A savage who observes our behavior and our ways is buried deep within each of us. . . . When we improve ourselves, when the spirit in us wakens, when our souls reign over our bodies, then the savage one within us sleeps. But, when we strive only for material goals, when we have no ideals, when our spirit sleeps, then the savage one awakens and forces us to go against civilization, against the laws of humanity!" ("Vos? Vu iz der vilder mentsh? Der vilder mentsh zitst tif bagrobn bay yedn fun unz, betrakht alle unzer benemen, unzer oyffirung. . . . Ven mir bildn zikh, ven der gayst ervakht in unz, ven unzer zele hersht iber'n kerper, dan shloft in unz der vilder mentsh, ober farkert, ven vir shtrebn nur tsu matiriele tsiln, ven vir hobn kayne idealn, ven unzer gayst shloft, dan vakht in unz der vilder mentsh, velkher tsvingt unz tsu geyn gegn tsivilizatsion, gegn di gezetse der mentshhayt.") This analysis of one who would fall prey to the animal instinct within him perfectly describes Gregor as he is shown to have been before the metamorphosis: a man of few ideals, devoted single-mindedly to material gain. His mother unwittingly reveals the paucity of his previous existence: "The boy thinks about nothing but his work." ("Der Junge hat ja nichts im Kopf als das Geschäft.") Even the one ideal that Gregor seems to have lived for—his plan to send his sister to the music conservatory—is presented in terms of money ("despite the great expense that would entail, which must be made up in some other way"). ("Ohne Rücksicht auf die grossen Kosten, die das verursachen musste, und die man schon auf andere Weise hereinbringen würde.")

Gordin's play warns of the "beast" lurking in every man beneath the human facade. Similarly, Kafka seems to be pointing to the vermin which every man inherently embodies. While most readers will not be ready to accept Gregor as a universal symbol of man, it is difficult to escape the conclusion that in *The Metamorphosis* Kafka is portraying what was, at least at that time, his own despairing, tragicomic vision of the human condition.

The Metamorphosis

Ronald Gray

The other story written in the autumn of 1912, after the meeting with Felice
Bauer, was written in circumstances quite different from those of "The Judgment." Earlier, Kafka had been delighted at the steady flow of creation
throughout the night. *The Metamorphosis* (originally translated as "The Transformation"), by contrast, took almost three weeks, from November 18 to
December 6, with interruptions on several evenings. For the first time, Kafka
was able to hold a conception of some length and complexity over a period
of weeks, and maintain its composition through to the end. This is the longest
by far of all his completed works, and the only one in which the formal
achievement is really important. Unlike any other of his stories, it is divided
into three equal sections, each headed by a Roman numeral like an act of
a play, each section ending with a climactic moment. In the first, Gregor
Samsa awakens to the realisation that he has turned into an insect and emerges
from his bedroom, to be driven back by his infuriated father. In the second,
he tries to accommodate himself to his absurdly hideous predicament, while
his sister offers him various foods, doing all she can to reconcile herself and
the family to the monster he has become; again, a brief sally into the living
room is repulsed by the father, this time even more violently, as he pelts
Gregor with apples. In the third, Gregor comes out while his sister is playing the violin, entranced by the music which seems to be the "food" he has
so long been unable to find, but a third attack drives him back to die alone
and untended. The family (excepting the father) having done all they can
with their varying limitations, to acclimatise themselves, or to offer comfort

---

From *Franz Kafka.* © 1973 by Cambridge University Press.

and love, finally recognise their failure. After Gregor's death they turn with relief to the happier life that now awaits them.

Kafka was usually reluctant to have anything he had written published, and this remained true of *The Metamorphosis*: he declined Kurt Wolff's invitation to send it to him in April 1913, perhaps because Kafka intended it for a book planned long before, to be entitled "Sons." He did, however, send it in 1914 to the novelist Robert Musil, who accepted it for the *Neue Rundschau*, where it would have appeared but for opposition from the conservative management. And in the following year he came as near as he ever did come to urging a publisher to print a work of his, saying he was "particularly concerned" to see publication. Considering Kafka's normal hesitancy, this suggests a strong feeling that the story came up to his expectations.

The formal excellence is striking enough in itself. Whereas very many of the stories are incomplete (including a large number of fragmentary beginnings in the diary, not normally printed in collections of the stories as such), or rambling and repetitive, *The Metamorphosis* shows all the signs that Kafka was able both to portray his own situation and to achieve artistic mastery over it. That this is Kafka's situation, as he saw it, need not be doubted. He himself comments on the similarity between the name Samsa and his own, noting that this time he has come closer than he did in the case of Bendemann. The parents and the sister correspond closely to his view of his family, though only his sister Ottla seems to be included, and the sisters Elli and Vally are left out. It remains, of course, a projection from his own circumstances as much as any autobiographical subject in a novel does. The distinctive feature is the device by which Kafka omits all the repetitive doubts, the neurotic self-circlings, packing them all into the one image of the transformation, and viewing that as though from the outside. The transformation is at first sight incomprehensible, without some experience of it through Kafka's diaries. Yet it remains the obvious and most compelling image for his condition, as he saw it, and there is no symbolism about it, or rather the metaphorical element seems so slight, so ordinary, so much a matter of everyday speech that one scarcely wants to translate when Gregor discovers himself to be *ein Ungeziefer* (a word which means "vermin," rather than "insect"). Gregor is, as one says, a louse. Nor does Kafka allow the comfort which might come from the expectation that the whole affair is a dream from which there will be an awakening. Exceptionally, there is no quality of dreams in this nightmare. Kafka insists on what the reader knows to be a physical impossibility, even though the general idea is common enough, because that is the only way that the full weight of his meaning can be conveyed, without overloading the story with the minutiae of self-recrimination. The conviction of being verminous is given full statement, once and for all, on the first page, and the rest becomes a matter of working out the practical details so that the truth comes home in concrete form.

This conviction is not the conviction of humanity at large, nor does the story ever make it out to be so; the implications exist for Gregor alone, and the rest of the characters are far from thinking themselves or being vermin. The notion that there is here what a recent school-edition described as "an ultimately serious and universally human parable of man's fate" (Kafka, *Die Verwandlung*, ed. M. L. Hoover) though obscurely conveyed in those words, seems to rest on a preconception that all men find themselves utterly repulsive, or should do. A not very different idea is expressed by another commentator, who finds here an exposure of the "persistent primitiveness of man" (F. D. Luke, "The Metamorphosis," in *Franz Kafka Today*). "Shall we not say that the bug is better, more oneself," writes Paul Goodman, "than the commercial traveller or the official in the insurance office?" and again, more emphatically, "the animal-identity is deeper than the ordinary human being and his behaviour, it is nearer to the unknown deity . . ." (Preface to *The Metamorphosis by Franz Kafka*). To deny this is not to remove all possible sympathy with Kafka's story, it is to maintain a sense of proportion. The cliché which says that every novelist worth his salt is normally describing Everyman is too persistent.

The really significant thing is the control which Kafka gains by stating his own condition, nobody else's, so simply. One of the principal advantages thus won is that, the interminable and inconclusive debates of later stories being excluded, he is able to take in the feelings and reactions of other people. The humanity which is lacking in some of the other stories, especially in "In the Penal Colony," is more in evidence in *The Metamorphosis*. The concentration on the *alter ego* who is the central character goes with a concentration in his relationship to the rest, simply because his condition is accepted without demur. What tenacity of will this acceptance implies needs little comment.

The whole story is worked out in terms of Gregor being an insect and at no point does the reader have the sense of being slyly invited to see more than meets the eye. There are no enigmas in the dialogue, to be resolved (as in "The Judgment") only by reference to Kafka's own life; though his life is latently present throughout, it is independent of the story and allows it to proceed without hindrance. At times in Kafka's writing he suggests compassion through some artificial device, as he does in "A Hunger-Artist." In *The Metamorphosis* there are no devices, and the compassion is felt in the writing. It is not simply that the sister, confronted with an impossible situation, attempts the impossible in caring for the insect her brother has become, though the implications of that are moving in themselves. The love Gregor feels for her is in the rhythm of the prose, as when he hears her play the violin in the presence of the three lodgers. It is even more clearly present in the passage where Gregor's father starts throwing apples at him. The emotion mounts to a climax in which the urgency of the mother's pleading is as strongly present as the desperation of Gregor himself.

> The little red apples rolled around on the floor as though magnetised, cannoning into one another. An apple thrown without much force grazed Gregor's back, but slid off without harm. Another, following immediately after it, however, sank deep into Gregor's back. Gregor tried to drag himself forward, as if the astounding, unbelievable pain might change if he moved to another place, but he felt as though he were nailed down, and flattened himself out in complete derangement of all his senses. The last thing he saw was the door of his room being flung open and his mother, followed by his shrieking sister, rushing in in her slip, as his sister had undressed her to let her breathe freely after her swoon, and then rushing up to his father, her petticoats falling down one after another, stumbling over the petticoats and hurling herself on his father, embracing him, in complete union with him—here Gregor's sight was already failing—and with her hands clasped at the back of his father's head, pleading with him to spare Gregor's life.

Strangest of all passages in Kafka, this has his double edge in its most notable form. There is surely some human sympathy here, in the portrayal of the mother, one wants to say, yet the thought of Kafka's avowed, detachment from the emotions his readers were likely to feel, the calculating element in him, gives cause for doubt. "An apple thrown without much force"? It sounds over-nonchalant when an insect is the target, and so does the interest in the behavior of the apples on the floor. Is there a paradox present, or is the mood simply one of detachment? A touch of humour is noticeable even in the tragic situation. It is partly due to the petticoats falling down, partly something slightly stylised in the way the mother beseeches the father— "beseeches" is the word, it has just that faint touch of the melodramatic, and the mother's hands grasping the back of the father's head also have a classic, and therefore stylised simplicity. Certain overtones also appear, especially in the reference to Gregor's being "nailed down" (*festgenagelt*) and, differently, in the coup de grace of his seeing his mother and father perfectly united— the one sight he would have preferred not to see—at the moment that his eyesight dims. But above all there is the breathless rise to a climax, grotesque in the circumstances when one realises what kind of creature is being protected, and the urgency of *Schonung* ("sparing"), uttered with the mother's own intensity. Yet the whole is shot through with that mystical dissociation that actually allows a humorous note to accompany every moment.

A similar paradoxical mood characterises the moment of Gregor's death; not in itself, for the description here has nothing ironical or melodramatic, but in its context, in the events which follow immediately on it. Left alone in his room with the apple festering on him, he feels his strength ebb:

> "And what now?" Gregor thought to himself, and looked round in the darkness. He quickly discovered that he was unable to move at all now. He was not surprised at that, it seemed unnatural to him that he should actually have been able to get about up to this moment on these frail little legs. And on the whole he did feel relatively comfortable. He had pains all over his body, it was true, but he felt they were gradually becoming weaker and weaker, and would in the end disappear completely. The rotting apple in his back and the inflammation round it, covered with dirty fluff, scarcely troubled him. He thought again of his family with affection and love. His feeling that he had to vanish from the face of the earth was, if possible, stronger than his sister's. In this state of vacant, peaceful contemplation he remained, until the tower clock struck three in the morning. He was just conscious of the first brightening of the sky outside his window. Then, without his willing it, his head sank to the floor, and his last breath passed faintly through his nostrils.

There is no such moment as this anywhere else in Kafka, no such calm recognition of what was a reality of his own condition. He is convinced here that Gregor must disappear from the face of the earth, and the conviction has no resentment in it, nor has it any expectation of Gregor's being rewarded by some dialectical reversal of fortunes. Unlike Leverkühn in Mann's *Doktor Faustus*, Gregor is not speculating on being a particularly attractive morsel for divine Grace to snap at; the story is basically humanistic, atheistic, unconcerned about divine sanction or resurrection. Considering the savagery with which "In the Penal Colony" describes a death without prospect of benefit, the calm of *The Metamorphosis* is surprising. On the other hand, it is not a passage to which one can do more than assent. There is no other way out for Gregor, it is true, so far as one can see from the story. Yet "vacant, peaceful contemplation" is not particularly admirable, and the general sense is of a feeble rather than a serene calm.

It is not a calm proudly presented for inspection. As soon as Gregor's death has passed, Kafka allows the charwoman, one of his best comic creations, to burst in. The reaction she shows is inhuman if one still regards Gregor as a human being. But that is the point: for the charwoman Gregor is not a human being; he is an insect and always has been. In allowing her to show such indifference Kafka does, it is true, indicate that the attempt of the sister at bridging the gap between herself and Gregor is vain. The story has this utterly pessimistic note, so far as Gregor is concerned, but the reader who finds this assertion of a human being's unloveableness unbearable may have to see that it is also ineluctable. Gregor must vanish, and the charwoman is chosen to say so:

> When the charwoman came, early in the morning, — out of sheer energy and impatience she slammed every single door, for all that she had been continually asked not to, so that from the moment she arrived there was no possibility of sleeping anywhere in the whole flat — she at first found nothing special in her first customary, cursory visit to Gregor. She thought he was lying so motionless on purpose, playing at being insulted; she credited him with every conceivable kind of intelligence. Happening to have the long broom in her hand, she tried tickling Gregor from the door. Obtaining no success that way either, she became annoyed and shoved at Gregor a little, and only when she had pushed him from where he lay without the least resistance did she begin to take notice. Quickly seeing how things stood, she opened her eyes wide, whistled to herself, but did not take long before she had flung open the door of the bedroom and shouted into the darkness at the top of her voice, "Come and have a look, it's done for, lying there done for it is!"

Kafka could only have written in that way of an inner certainty which recognised the crude life of the charwoman as decidedly as he recognised his own nature, or the dominant aspect of his own nature. The charwoman sweeps back into the scene like something out of a comic postcard, a self-sufficient bull of a woman, although as she does so, a critical reservation in Kafka's mind begins to make itself felt. He is not writing here a story on the lines of Mann's *Tonio Kröger*, where there is such an abject surrender to the spirit of the triumphant "Bürger." Gregor is dead, but the victory is not with the opposition. There is a certain comedy already in the slight hesitation shown by the charwoman about opening such a thing as a bedroom door early in the morning, and this now develops into a further not wholly serious situation, as Herr and Frau Samsa, woken by her shouting, get out of bed symmetrically. This is kept up in the description of the three lodgers—a main source of comedy in the story (and perhaps derived from the four Buffers in *Our Mutual Friend*)—who act with the perfect uniformity of the decent, convention-respecting man. They take their hats from the hat-stand, their sticks from the umbrella-stand, all at the same moment, they bow, and go down the stairs; reappearing at regular intervals as the landings hide them or bring them into view. One sees here Kafka's ironical reserve, working from a point of view well behind the horrifying persona with which he had to live. The "Bürger," to use Thomas Mann's term, may have vitality and robustness, but he has the absurdity of an automaton. The victory does not belong to him, and there is no talk of reconciliation between him and anything that Gregor stands for.

This is still not the end of Kafka's comment; amusing as these moments are (if one can see them from out of his wretched state), they offer more light relief than social criticism. They are not penetrating, and the "Bürger" is not really to be so easily dismissed. There remains the final scene when, Gregor being dead, the family is at last free of him and decides, since it is springtime, to take a tram-ride for an excursion into the country. The last sentences have some of Kafka's best cadences as well as his fullest vision:

> While they were conversing like this, it occurred almost at the same moment to Herr and Frau Samsa, seeing their daughter's vitality return more and more strongly, that despite the sorrow which had brought a pallor to her cheeks she had recently blossomed into a pretty girl with an attractive figure.
>
> Falling silent, and almost unconsciously exchanging understanding glances, they reflected that it would soon be time to be finding a proper young man for her. And it was like a confirmation of their fresh dreams and good intentions when, as they arrived at the end of their journey, their daughter rose to her feet first and stretched her young body.

This is Kafka most fully in possession of himself as a writer. The verminous self must go: it has no hold on life, and no destiny but extinction. On the other hand, the brave new world now emerges, not unsatirised: the parents are still slightly uniform and symmetrical, and such good intentions as they may have are coloured by the half-conscious, and presumably calculating glances they exchange, their minds half-fixed on what advantages a suitor may bring.

But the story does end with that glimpse of a woman ready for love and marriage; there are subtleties and simplicities here of a human order.

The ending was the one part of the story Kafka could not approve. At the moment he finished it he wrote to Felice to tell her so, adding, "only the ending as it is today doesn't make me feel glad, it could have been better, there's no doubt." Whether he had anything specific in mind is impossible to say; he very seldom did make specific criticisms of his work. Not much more than a year later, he again rejected the ending, and perhaps the whole story with it: "Great dislike of 'Metamorphosis.' Unreadable ending. Imperfect almost to the very bottom. It would have been better if I had not been disturbed by the business trip" (*Diaries*). Unlike his objections to *America*, this did not prevent him from trying to get the story published. Did he dislike the momentary suggestion of an optimistic conclusion with its possible insincerity (as it probably was, for him)? What he had written was, all the same, more subtle than mere optimism would have been. And it was in any case a very brief escape. In *The Metamorphosis* he had seen his own existence as though from outside, in its relation with other lives, and though there was always another self which watched this self, he had recognised the need for this self to die. It was a personal affair, and he made no more of it than that, in this story. Had he realised the implications, he might never have written in the same vein again.

Within a short while, however, the conviction that his own state could represent a universal fact of existence entered his consciousness, and the stories he wrote after this are given a more general symbolic value. It seems very likely that his reading of Kierkegaard had something to do with this, for it was not until August 21, 1913, a year after the meeting with Felice, that he first read him, to judge by his diary entry for that day:

> "I received today Kierkegaard's 'Book of the Judge.' As I already sensed, despite essential differences his case is very like my own, at least he is on the same side of the world. He confirms me like a friend."

This was an important moment in Kafka's life. The isolated state he had always been in now appeared to him mirrored in another man's existence, a man who had gone through much the same crisis in relation to the woman he had intended to marry (Kierkegaard deliberately sacrificed his love for Regine Olsen) and whose father had meant as much to him spiritually as Kafka's had to him. From Kierkegaard he could have taken the view that the condition of his own mind was that of all men who had experienced dread, in the sense of awareness of infinite guilt, and he could have gained the impression, or had his impression confirmed, that this was a proper state for all men to be in. The fact is that, though there is nothing directly to suggest religious or generalising tendencies in the stories and novels begun before 1913, the first to follow after the reading of Kierkegaard showed them very clearly.

Die *Verwandlung*, Freud, and the Chains of Odysseus

David Eggenschwiler

For nearly half a century, since Hellmuth Kaiser's 1931 essay in *Imago*, Kafka's *Die Verwandlung* [*The Metamorphosis*] has been an obviously rich subject for psychoanalytic critics, from the most casual, who merely note its dreamlike qualities and Oedipal tussles, to the most persistent, who translate all of its symbolic odds and ids. Such inevitable interpretations have called for the equally inevitable reactions from the opponents of psychoanalytic criticism, who charge reductionism and the neglect of aesthetic values. So Gregor has become a test case, forced to carry on his spindly legs an increasing burden of controversy. I would hesitate to add another straw except in the hope of resolving some of the controversy and showing that the concerns of Freudian and formalist must converge in this story, that they are not merely equal but also inseparable. It will not do to keep an aloof toleration of various critical methods or even to combine approaches in a loose mixture, moving back and forth from manifest to latent content, trying to satisfy both Apollo and Dionysus in a mad rush from temple to temple. In this story the two gods consort in a most disturbing and amusing way.

The origin of *Die Verwandlung* came almost two months before its conception, in another literary "birth," as Kafka described it. On the night of September 22–23, 1912, in one eight-hour sitting, he wrote "Das Urteil" ["The Judgment"], the most important story he had written to that time, and the next day he rejoiced in his diary:

From *Modern Language Quarterly* 39, no. 4 (December 1978). © 1979 by the University of Washington. The translations have been appended by the editor.

Die fürchterliche Anstrengung und Freude, wie sich die Geschichte
vor mir entwickelte, wie ich in einem Gewässer vorwärtskam.
Mehrmals in dieser Nacht trug ich mein Gewicht auf dem Rücken.
Wie alles gesagt werden kann, wie für alle, für die fremdesten
Einfälle ein grosses Feuer bereitet ist, in dem sie vergehn und
auferstehn. . . . *Nur* so kann geschrieben werden, nur in einem
solchen Zusammenhang, mit solcher vollständigen Öffnung des
Leibes und der Seele.

[The fearful strain and joy, how the story developed before me,
as if I were advancing over water. Several times during this night
I heaved my own weight on my back. How everything can be
said, how for everything, for the strangest fancies, there waits
a great fire in which they perish and rise up again. . . . Only *in
this way* can writing be done, only with such coherence, with such
a complete opening out of the body and the soul.]

(*The Diaries of Franz Kafka 1910–1913*, edited by Max Brod, and translated
by Joseph Kresh. All further references will be to *Tagebücher* [*Diaries*].)

It is quite understandable that he felt such a release in this rush of
composition and that months later, while reading the proofs, he described
the story as having been born covered with filth and slime (*Tagebücher*). "Das
Urteil" is the most obviously confessional piece of fiction he ever wrote, Georg
Bendemann's ambivalent feelings about his father — aggression, fear, disgust,
guilt, love, competition — correspond exactly to the feelings Kafka claims to
have had about his own father, and the story reads like a transparent Oedipal
fantasy. Kafka himself realized the obvious psychological qualities, for he
wrote in his diary: "Viele während des Schreibens mitgeführte Gefühle, zum
Beispiel die Freude, dass ich etwas Schönes für Maxens 'Arkadia' haben werde,
Gedanken an Freud natürlich." ["Many emotions carried along in the writing,
joy, for example, that I shall have something beautiful for Max's *Arkadia*,
thoughts about Freud, of course."] (*Tagebücher*). Unlike Kafka's later works,
"Das Urteil" seems less a parable than a psychological fable with overt and
straightforward themes. As Erich Heller has written, "Never before or after,
it seems, has Freud ruled so supremely over a piece of literature." But the
revolution was already at hand, for within two months Kafka would begin
Die Verwandlung, in which he would treat similar psychological themes in
ways that examine and debate what the earlier story naively represented. Freud's
supreme reign was soon followed by a democratic republic.

Kafka's jottings about psychology form a useful background for *Die Verwandlung.* Opponents of psychoanalytic criticism too readily seize on his brief outbursts in his octavo notebooks ("Zum letzenmal Psychologie!" ["Never again psychology!"] or "Übelkeit nach zuviel Psychologie" ["Nausea after too much psychology"] [*Dearest Father: Stories and Other Writings,* translated by Ernst Kaiser and Eithne Wilkens. All further references will be to *Dearest Father.*]) to show that he soon rejected the whole business. But some of his comments show a more balanced, and at times brilliant, view of contemporary psychology. His most perceptive statements are entered in his notebooks for October 19, 1917:

> Es gibt keine Beobachtung der innern Welt, so wie es eine der äussern gibt. Zumindest deskriptive Psychologie ist wahrscheinlich in der Gänze ein Anthropomorphismus, ein Ausragen der Grenzen. Die innere Welt lässt sich nur leben, nicht beschreiben. —Psychologie ist die Beschreibung der Spiegelung der irdischen Welt in der himmlischen Fläche oder richtiger: die Beschreibung einer Spiegelung, wie wir, Vollgesogene der Erde, sie uns denken, denn eine Spiegelung erfolgt gar nicht, nur wir sehen Erde. wohin wir uns auch wenden.

> Psychologie ist Ungeduld.

> Alle menschlichen Fehler sind Ungeduld, ein vorzeitiges Abbrechen des Methodischen, ein scheinbares Einpfählen der scheinbaren Sache.

> [There is no such thing as observation of the inner world, as there is of the outer world. At least descriptive psychology is probably, taken as a whole, a form of anthropomorphism, a nibbling at our own limits. The inner world can only be experienced, not described —Psychology is the description of the reflection of the terrestrial world in the heavenly plane, or, more correctly, the description of a reflection such as we, soaked as we are in our terrestrial nature, imagine it, for no reflection actually occurs, only we see the earth wherever we turn.

> Psychology is impatience.

All human errors are impatience, the premature breaking off of
what is methodical, an apparent fencing in of the apparent thing.]

("Hochzeitsvorbereitungen" ["Wedding Preparations"])

If we were to understand "Psychologie" to refer to an older Lockean, instead
of Freudian, theory, would this not sound, in style and content, like something
from Blake's notebooks? So history turns upon itself as poets challenge scien-
tists. But even as Blake eventually found a necessary, if largely antagonistic,
role for Newton and Locke in his visionary apocalypse, so Kafka found a
useful and carefully limited role for Freud in his own experience of the inner
world. In the last part of the passage from the notebooks, he accuses psychology
of what we now call reductionism, of too strong a desire to formulate, simplify,
explain in terms of basic concepts. But in saying that it prematurely breaks
off, he says, not that it is on the wrong path, but that it is too impatient
to reach the goal and so mistakenly accepts partial answers for complete ones.
Of course for Kafka (as for Blake) one can never reach final insight — ("Es
gibt ein Ziel, aber keinen Weg") ["There is a goal, but no way"] ["Hochzeitsvorbereitungen"] — but one must journey; one must not worship false gods
by mistaking a part for the whole, a stage of the journey for its end. And
a proper view of psychology can help to show the way and to reveal the
limits at which we nibble in our search.

    If this last part of Kafka's entry is intelligent and explicit, the first part
is brilliant, suggestive, and even more to our purposes. By calling psychology
a form of anthropomorphism, Kafka claims that through it the conscious
mind projects its own image onto the inner world; while thinking that it
is describing the entire self, that mind is actually describing its own features.
The subsequent analogy of the terrestrial falsely reflected in the heavenly extends the religious connotations of anthropomorphism and implies that the
inner world is sacred. Thus psychology pretends to describe in rational and
observably human images an inner world that is indescribable, irrational, and
inhuman; it profanes the sacred and makes the mysterious seem knowable.
It lies to us, but it might tell us, soaked as we are in our terrestrial nature,
what we want to hear, perhaps what we need to hear if we are to carry
on our human commerce in a world that otherwise would be full of terrors.
What, though, if one were to awaken from uneasy dreams to find that one
no longer had a human form? How could the rational mind deal with that
failure of anthropomorphism? And how could we, reading an account of
such a thing, explain that impossible metamorphosis in terms that make it
comprehensible, that apparently fence in the apparent thing and give the story,
if not the creature, a human form? And how might an author who is wise

and skeptical about an anthropomorphic psychology lead us to examine our own needs and illusions? We have, it seems, good cause to be wary in our assumptions about Kafka and psychology.

So Gregor Samsa, hard-working salesman, dutiful son, quiet home-body, awakes one morning to find that he has been transformed into a gigantic insect (or a monstrous vermin or a monstrous bug or, in any case, "einem ungeheueren Ungeziefer"). If the rest of the story sustained this potential element of fairy tale or surrealistic fantasy, we could easily accept this opening incident as part of a genre in which such suspensions of natural law are everyday occurrences, requiring a ready suspension of disbelief so that we could enter the fabulous province. But, as most readers and critics have testified, the realistic form of the story after the opening sentence will not allow us to adjust our expectations so comfortably. Because the humdrum world that Gregor inhabits is not an appropriate setting for such nocturnal metamorphoses, we (if not the characters) cast about for an explanation, and literature as well as literary criticism has taught us that such incidents might well be considered symbolic, especially when they so emphatically interrupt a realistic surface and thus imply special significances, figurative meanings when literal ones seem so inadequate.

Kafka, writing this story only two months after "Das Urteil," invites us to turn psychological as, in passage after passage, he supplies the most obvious grist for the Freudian mill. Why else does he give such a prominent place in his second paragraph to the picture of a woman in furs that Gregor has cut out of a magazine and put in a special frame he has spent his evenings making? And why does Kafka stylistically mark that passage with the odd comment that the woman's whole forearm had vanished ("verschwunden war") into her muff, as though such a disappearance were uncanny rather than commonplace? Since we are indirectly given Gregor's point of view here as he looks about his room, apparently the attention to, and impressions of, the furry woman are his, and she is the first thing to which he turns his attention after seeing his insect's body. Soon, of course, he thinks of his tiring job, his demanding schedule, his sacrifices for his parents, his employer who sits on high and talks down intimidatingly to his employees. When one combines these initial thoughts with Gregor's strong appetite this morning, his preference for garbage over fresh food, and the pleasure and relief he feels in abandoning an upright posture to crawl, even over ceiling and walls with extraordinary agility, one may well conclude—as many critics have—that the metamorphosis symbolizes a rebellious assertion of unconscious desires and energies, the primitive and infantile demands of the id. Gregor soon implies as much and also provides a complementary interpretation when he suggests that he has been driven mad and made unable to leave his bed because he is conscience-stricken over wasting even an hour of his firm's time. Thus one might conclude that the transformation symbolizes both a libidinous rebellion and a condemnation of such rebellion, even of unconscious desires to rebel. Simultaneously, Gregor, poor bewildered simpleton, is caught between psychological forces that are either too immoral or too moral. Fortunately psychoanalytic theory, with its condensations and reversals, can accommodate such contradictory meanings of a symbol: that dexterity is one of its most charming means of making perplexing things coherent, as Kafka knew when he wrote ironically in his notebooks: "was das immer stimmende Resultat betrifft, ergebnisreich" ["as regards the always correct result, it is richly informative"] ("Hochzeitsvorbereitungen"). It is always correct because it is a self-validating system with its own means of explaining away objections that are not derived from its premises. That is why it is such a useful and reassuring method for explaining the monstrous transformation of Gregor into vermin. It can accommodate such a multeity of significances into its unity. If we allow the context of "Das Urteil" into our speculations, it can even explain that, like Georg Bendemann's sentence of death, the metamorphosis signifies guilt and the desire for punishment for having usurped the father's role (as well as signifying guilt for wanting to abandon that tiresome role). And, for a final reversal, it can demonstrate a desire for aggression against the supplanted father and the other figures of authority associated with his primal power.

A patient reading of Stanley Corngold's summary of articles and chapters on the story will show that all of these interpretations have been offered by commentators, although not often in such profusion. And there are good reasons why such explanations should be common: the obtrusively obvious images and actions, the patent juxtaposition of symbols with descriptions of Gregor's longing, frustrations, and guilt, even the coy asides that suggest a psychological possibility while pretending to deny it — these techniques coax from the reader a psychological interpretation. And if the reader were to consider Kafka's personal writings (including a contemporaneous letter to Max Brod in which he told of a near suicide to escape a conflict analogous to Gregor's) and preceding fiction (including "Das Urteil" and "Hochzeitsvorbereitungen auf dem Lande," in which a character desires to send his clothed body into the world while he remains in bed as a large beetle), if, that is, the reader were to consider contexts likely to determine intention and validate interpretation, why then he might well have "Gedanken an Freud natürlich" ["thoughts about Freud, of course" (Tagebücher)]. About this story, however, those thoughts should be complicated with irony.

Throughout the first two parts of the story Kafka repeatedly and brilliantly confounds our responses by first encouraging a symbolic interpretation and then dropping us uncomfortably into literal fact. By a sophisticated form of romantic irony he dislocates our critical point of view. For example, when Gregor's sister and mother are removing his furniture in order to give him more crawling space, he suddenly realizes that he is losing his human past, and, as a gesture of opposition, he places himself over the picture of the woman described so obtrusively in the opening paragraphs. His choice of human object seems inevitable for a psychological reading; he is momentarily trying to preserve a symbol of his sexually repressed and socially acceptable past in order to resist further surrender to the primitive instincts that are controlling him. But what are we then to make of the comment that the glass of the picture "ihn festhielt und seinem heissen Bauch wohltat" ["was a good surface to hold on to and comforted his hot belly (*Bauch*)"] (*Franz Kafka: The Complete Stories*, edited by Nahum N. Glatzer, translated by Willa and Edwin Muir. All further references will be to *The Complete Stories*)? This comment does not thematically contradict the psychological reading; if we were tactlessly persistent, we could even mutter something about sublimations cooling the overheated id. But these tactile images do something more effective; they jar us out of the symbolic mode and into the world of the literal vermin. They make us imagine in an awful moment what it would be like to have human sensations (is a bug comforted by being cooled?) through the body of a gigantic insect conceived in partly human terms (does a bug have a belly, *Bauch*, rather than the entomological *Hinterleib*?). Of course a symbolic reading should not try to account for every description in the text, but, if it is to remain confident, it cannot afford to be challenged so strikingly by incongruous, juxtaposed details. And Kafka challenges it often in this manner. He sends Gregor across the walls to hang from the ceiling in almost blissful absorption; and we recognize in these acrobatics a new freedom even in Gregor's confinement, a feeling of release and pleasure in his inhuman agility, a rising above the plane of his old, routine life. (And Kafka, to his shame, was such a poor gymnast, whereas his father was proudly athletic.) Then we are shown the sticky traces Gregor leaves behind, traces that do not come from the subconscious: they are repulsively entomological, not psychological. They befoul our symbols as well as Gregor's once-human room.

Not all of the shifts in perspective are so gruesome: some even contribute to the humor of the tale. Has not every reader noted the amusingly strange nonchalance with which Gregor at first accepts his metamorphosis? That strangeness corresponds to the incongruities I have been discussing. On the one hand, we have Gregor's reasonable attempts to explain his new state as nonsense or as fantasy or as delusion caused by the hyperactive conscience of a dutiful employee. We could add other explanations, but even if we consider the metamorphosis as literary symbolism rather than delusion, we would still be imitating Gregor's attempts to explain the literal change as somehow unreal, as metaphorical. On the other hand, Gregor also applies his calm reason to problems of manipulating this unfamiliar body in which his consciousness is encased. This switching of hands causes comic non sequiturs when Gregor first decides that after he has gotten out of bed the fantasy will disappear, then spends much mental and physical effort trying to operate the unknown mechanisms of this supposedly unreal body in order to get up so that the body will prove unreal. And around he goes, from a detached perspective (this body does not literally exist) to an immanent one (how does one work these writhing little legs?). Because Kafka gives us vivid accounts of the body and Gregor's frustrating attempts to manipulate it, we too are wrenched from one perspective to another, from symbol to fact, with what should be amused perplexity. How else could we at one moment consider solemn psychological interpretations and at the next witness a scene of awful and amusing slapstick in which Gregor muddles on with the same kind of deadpan stoicism with which Buster Keaton and Charlie Chaplin endure the intolerably inhuman obstacles that surround them? Psychoanalytic theory might explain such humor as defensive screening, but it would thereby trivialize the problem with its self-validating formula; it would supply an unconscious cause for the comic incongruities without considering their strong and subtle effects, their literary value and complex puposes. It would be reductive.

A still more obvious example of such double perspective is the scene in which Gregor first confronts his father, a confrontation that seems inescapably and intentionally Freudian. After Gregor has first emerged from his room and has caused the office manager to flee, he is set upon by his father, who grabs the manager's cane (symbol of authority and, if you will, a phallic flayer) and a newspaper, which Kimberly Sparks has convincingly shown to be also a symbol of authority (they who rule the house—Gregor, Mr. Samsa, the three boarders—sit at the head of the table and read the newspaper). The father drives Gregor before him, hissing like a savage ("wie ein Wilder"), and as Gregor nears his room, the sound becomes so loud that it no longer seems to him the voice of only one father ("gar nicht mehr wie die Stimme bloss eines einzigen Vaters"). A brandished cane, a savage, a multiplied father—the scene pushes irresistibly into a primal conflict, representing the unconscious infantile fears that Freud had already described in the famous and then highly controversial *Three Essays on the Theory of*

Sexuality, published in 1905. But at the same time we have another emotionally incongruous scene superimposed on this elemental struggle; we have a man chasing away a large bug in the way in which bugs and other unpleasant creatures are usually chased, by waving a newspaper, prodding with a stick, and hissing (shooing). This incongruity challenges us by refusing to allow an adequate response. Are we not to sympathize with Gregor in his confusion and fear, and are we not also to recognize the allusions that associate that fear with what Freud claimed to be a most elemental source of anxiety? We respond to the plight of the loathly son and undersand that it symbolically represents the plight of all sons. But our compassion and our understanding seem mocked by the opposing image of a man shooing away a bug. Can we be sure that we do not have a grotesque joke? And at whose expense would it be? And how much would it undercut the psychological themes? If, intellectually, the latent content is made almost too obvious by the manifest content, is it not, affectively, subverted by the manifest? In corresponding terms of literary analysis, the figurative meanings stated or implied in the scene that broaden its references (like a savage, like many fathers) are opposed in tone by some of the literal meanings. The symbolic collides with the matter-of-fact.

Kafka repeats this technique in the second confrontation between father and son, but this time makes the psychological symbolism so obvious that it approaches caricature. The mother has fainted in Gregor's room upon seeing her son; Gregor has rushed into the living room to help the sister secure aid; the sister has locked Gregor out of his room in which the mother still lies; and the father returns, finding the son interposed between him and his wife, pressed against the bedroom door. A pat tableau for the psychological climax, especially since we are now told that, in the times of Gregor's dominance in the family, the feeble father used to walk between mother and son in their daily strolls. As the physical positions are now reversed, so are the biological and psychological, for the dominant father is revitalized; he stands erect, his eyes dart under bushy eyebrows, and he wears a uniform with gold buttons (we might recall the photograph of Gregor from his army days: he stands there confident, smiling, with his hand on his sword, of all things). As the father approaches, Gregor is appropriately astonished at the enormous size of the soles of the father's shoes. While they circle the room, the father begins his deadly assault on his son: he begins throwing apples at him. As horrified as Gregor feels, as symbolic as this confrontation may be, the scene is a bit silly: the father filling his pockets from the fruit bowl and pitching the apples at his verminous son, the little red apples rolling about the floor as if magnetized and knocking into each other. The description suggests some kind of children's game. And if we are to take the apples as particularly symbolic, as some commentators have done without irony, the scene becomes even more ridiculous. If these apples have been imported from Eden and if they symbolize the instrument by which the original Father expelled his son from paradise, then Kafka has turned *Moses and Monotheism* into a travesty a quarter of a century before it was written. But one need not seek so obscurely for parody of Freud. No sooner is Gregor wounded and made to feel nailed ("festgenagelt") to the spot (perhaps making him Christ as well as Adam in this biblical collage) than his mother, dressed in her chemise, breaks from his bedroom, embraces the father in complete union with him ("in gänzlicher Vereinigung mit ihm"), and begs for her son's life. That is a primal scene with a vengeance. It is no wonder that the son's sight fails at this point. Commentators who write only of Gregor's exclusion here from the complete union of the family group seem willfully unpsychological, but those who merely point out its Oedipal character without considering its tone and parodic nature seem willfully unliterary. As Gregor reaches the climax of his Freudian drama, Kafka pulls out all stops and plays a wonderfully loud and heavy-handed variation on the Oedipal themes he has used throughout. Here, no more indirection, no more allusion, no more symbol, but the veritable primal scene *an sich.*

The brassy crescendo that ends section 2 all but ends Kafka's use of Freudian themes in his treatment of Gregor; as we shall soon see, these themes will be redistributed in the Samsa family to different effects. Necessarily, then, except for a brief reappearance in section 3, it also ends the ironic use he has made of Gregor's verminous body to suggest and to undercut psychoanalytic themes. That technique of playing the literal against the symbolic corresponds generally to what Corngold has explained as Kafka's development of "ungeheueren Ungeziefer" ["gigantic insect"] as a distorted metaphor that is neither entirely figurative nor entirely literal (*The Commentators' Despair*). But whereas Corngold sees the subject of *Die Verwandlung* as language itself, I am concerned with that use of language to suggest the values and limits of psychology. Kafka's allusions and patterns do imply that psychology helps to specify the desires and fears of the inner life. And his use of inexplicable brute and brutal facts marks limits, implies that the inner life cannot be entirely known, entirely fenced in by anthropomorphic theories. Either to spell out a set of psychoanalytic patterns or to assert that Gregor's metamorphosis is entirely and intentionally incomprehensible is to miss the further pleasure of recognizing both and appreciating their interplay. In part 3 Kafka pointedly interrupts that interplay and by doing so clarifies his tale and further develops its power and its humor.

The changes of structure in the final part and the corresponding adjustments in symbolic method are acts of great intelligence. Kafka himself thought that the story should have been better constructed and should have had a more consistent style; but *Die Verwandlung,* with its multiple climaxes and changing structure, has a far more sophisticated and interesting form than "Das Urteil," which Kafka seemed to prefer. And the basic change in structure that occurs in section 3 makes possible a still more interesting critique of psychology than had been achieved in the first two sections.

Because Gregor has been decisively defeated and seriously wounded in his struggle, even the father is now reminded that Gregor is a member of the family ("ein Familienmitglied"); so the Samsas leave the son's door open in the evening. On the hinges of this opened door the story turns about thematically and structurally. By admitting that Gregor is one of them—although separated, in darkness, on the other side of the doorway—the Samsas begin to assume some of the burdens that have been symbolized by Gregor's metamorphosis. Throughout sections 1 and 2 the Samsas usually act singly or in pairs and almost always in direct relation to Gregor: the sister feeds Gregor and cleans his room; the sister and mother remove his furniture; the father struggles with him. At the beginning the three Samsas address Gregor in three different tones of voice (one gentle, one harsh, one imploratory) through three different doors. But in section 3 they always act as a group and seldom in direct relation to Gregor (except at their own psychological climax). These changes are revealing, for the three Samsas, acting now as the closely related parts of one unit, of one psychologically symbolic character, assume and struggle with many of the problems that Gregor once had. They become the central actors, or composite actor, in the Freudian drama. And because Gregor now becomes, in a psychological sense, the main symbol of what they experience in economic, social, and domestic relationships, they do not deal with him directly until their crisis, until they must confront all of their problems as represented by him. Until then, they turn their attention outward, enduring the symptoms of their essential problems, not facing and acting on the causes.

Meanwhile, Gregor waits and watches. His door, which has opened symbolically onto the family group, has opened literally as well. In a concise gesture, Kafka has combined symbol and fact to great narrative advantage. Because, until Gregor's death, the narrator's physical (if not always intellectual) point of view is limited to Gregor's, we need that open door so that we can observe the other Samsas for the first time as they deal with and endure the world in which they have become the main actors. What we see through that doorway is not the revitalized family that some commentators have too casually described as emerging once Gregor has been removed from his prematurely dominant position in the household. That revitalization will come, but not so directly, not so easily. We see a family that is exhausted and depressed from laboring at menial jobs—messenger, seamstress, salesgirl. They live much as Gregor did before his metamorphosis. Like him each of them could say "ach Gott . . . was für einen anstrengenden Beruf habe ich gewählt" ["Oh God . . . what an exhausting job I've picked on"] (*The Complete Stories*), like him they spend weary evenings at home in a spiritless routine; like him they labor under an economic and psychological debt, which the father incurred and the son later returned: and like him they feel only a distant possibility of release. How appropriate that Gregor, transformed into a monster under such circumstances, should now serve as a symbol of their frustration, servility, and sacrifice. In a passage of subtle and precise juxtapositions Kafka makes it clear that the monstrous vermin is more a representation than a literal cause of their state:

> Die grösste Klage war aber stets, dass man diese für die gegenwärtigen Verhältnisse allzu grosse Wohnung nicht verlassen konnte, da es hicht auszudenken war, wie man Gregor übersiedeln sollte. Aber Gregor sah wohl ein, dass es nicht nur die Rücksicht auf ihn war, welche eine Übersiedlung verhinderte, denn ihn hätte man doch in einer passenden Kiste mit ein paar Luftlöchern leicht transportieren können; was die Familie hauptsächlich vom Wohnungswechsel abhielt, war vielmehr die völlige Hoffnungslosigkeit und der Gedanke daran, dass sie mit einem Unglück geschlagen war, wie niemand sonst im ganzen Verwandten- und Bekanntenkreis. Was die Welt von armen Leuten verlangt, erfüllten sie bis zum äussersten, der Vater holte den kleinen Bankbeamten das Frühstück, die Mutter opferte sich für die Wäsche fremder Leute, die Schwester lief nach dem Befehl der Kunden hinter dem Pulte hin und her, aber weiter reichten die Kräfte der Familie schon nicht.

> [But what they lamented most was the fact that they could not leave the flat which was much too big for their present circumstances, because they could not think of any way to shift Gregor. Yet Gregor saw well enough that consideration for him was not the main difficulty preventing the removal, for they could have easily shifted him in some suitable box with a few air holes in it; what really kept them from moving into another flat was

rather their own complete hopelessness and the belief that they had been singled out for a misfortune such as had never happened to any of their relations or acquaintances. They fulfilled to the uttermost all that the world demands of poor people, the father fetched breakfast for the small clerks in the bank, the mother devoted her energy to making underwear for strangers, the sister trotted to and fro behind the counter at the behest of customers, but more than this they had not the strength to do.]

(The Complete Stories)

Although the passage may be indirectly limited to Gregor's point of view ("Aber Gregor sah wol ein . . ." ["Yet Gregor saw well enough . . ."]), the narrative tone makes it seem quite reliable, and it prepares us well to understand later changes in the family. The three Samsas blame their condition most of all on Gregor, although they emphasize the practical problem of moving the monster. We are immediately told, however, that the practical concern is mainly a pretense and that their hopelessness and sense of unusual misfortune keep them from trying to improve their lot. Does not the reader at this point assume that the great *Unglück* [misfortune] that has imprisoned them is Gregor's metamorphosis, which makes them feel shame, victimization, and powerlessness? And certainly the metamorphosis itself is one of their misfortunes. But the next sentence tells not of Gregor's debilitating presence, but of the family's servile jobs. Ruled by small clerks, strangers, and customers, this pretty bourgeois family that once had its own business has fallen into the laboring class, where its strength, pride, and independence are lost. As a composite character the Samsas are now dominated, as Gregor once was, by authorities who correspond in the social world to the father in the infantile (and later the repressed) world of the Freudian Oedipal drama.

Appropriately, the center of this fallen family is Mr. Samsa. As he had risen to savage, gigantic, and even uniformed power in vanquishing the apparently rebellious son, so now he has declined into the most pathetic of the three Samsas. Even his uniform, which was once a sign of power and authority in the battle of father and son, has become a sign of servility. As he sleeps exhausted in his armchair at home, he continues to wear that uniform, not as if he were the proud patriarch, but "als sei er immer zu seinem Dienste bereit und warte auch hier auf die Stimme des Vorgesetzten" ["as if he were ready for service at any moment and even here only at the beck and call of his superior"] *(The Complete Stories)*. The uniform undergoes its own metamorphosis as the old father nods in his chair and the women form a chorus of gentle lamentation.

To balance these scenes of naturalistic pathos and to prepare for the second reversal of the story, Kafka introduces three stylized boarders. If the plight of the three Samsas has not seemed clearly enough psychological to this point, the appearance of the *drei Zimmerherren* [three boarders] should change that, for they turn this part of the story into a Freudian comedy, both in its structure and in its tone. The three gentlemen are explicitly figures of authority, harsh judgment, and hostile power. They dominate the Samsas, sitting arrogantly at the dinner table, reading the newspaper (that sign of dominance), haughtily judging the food and the sister's violin playing, and demanding strict neatness in the household, especially in the kitchen (that source of primal pleasure). They live together in one bedroom, wear full beards, dress alike, and move together like Siamese triplets, with the middle boarder always acting as the leader and the two side men of this little troupe always acting and speaking in unison. It is no wonder that the more persistent psychoanalytic critics have identified this aggressive hairy trinity, especially considering its isosceles arrangement, as a symbol of the paternal genitals. But if we indulge in such specific naming of parts, we ought to do so playfully. If Kafka is consciously or unconsciously representing the dread father's phallus, we must credit him, at whatever psychic level he resides, with a sense of humor. Yet we need not talk of phallic symbols or superegos to understand the function of the boarders. Intimidating this servile family, the boarders represent all forms of authority, both internal and external, that dominate such poor and ashamed people. And they pointedly *represent* such powers, for they are such stylized puppets, acting out a caricature of social and psychological forces. Because they are so stylized, representative, and ridiculous, they can focus the Samsas' anxieties on limited and well-defined antagonists, and by clearly defining the problems they make possible rebellion and reversal.

The condition of the three Samsas has become very schematized. Superimposed upon, and representing, their general anxiety is a pair of contrasting symbols. In the dark bedroom, in the jumble of discarded furniture and filth, is the monstrous vermin, a grotesque, hidden part of the family, a sign of their shame and unworthiness. Controlling the well-cleaned living room are the boarders, who insist that the Samsas are shameful and inferior. The pattern, which reproduces in simplified form the conflicts of Gregor's earlier life, is quite obvious, and the climax of the Samsas' story makes it even more so since it brings together the symbols of shame and judgment, forcing the Samsas to act decisively if they are to survive.

When the boarders first see Gregor, they mock the Samsas, then angrily demand explanations, and finally give notice, refusing to pay for their lodging and threatening legal action. Now the Samsas reach the bottom of their despair, for they face still more financial hardship and a public recognition of their shame. In desperation Grete, the youngest and pluckiest of the three, exclaims that the thing must go, that they must stop thinking that it is Gregor. Her outcry is climactic; it changes the Samsas' situation as decisively as the thrown apples had changed Gregor's. During the night Gregor dies. In the morning the Samsas discover the death, retire to the parents' room where they weep, then emerge to confront and banish the peevish boarders. The psychological pattern is again obvious: by a desperate act of will the Samsas have refused to believe any longer that the vermin is part of themselves; they have disclaimed their guilt and unworthiness by reversing the gesture of acceptance with which section 3 and the account of their suffering began. When they have refused to be overwhelmed by shame and hopelessness, the symbol of those feelings disappears, and they can banish the figures who have judged them.

If this were all there were to it, the climax of the story would be as thin and uninteresting as the above summary. But the psychological scheme is realized so well in ways that give interesting perspectives on the scheme itself. We must put aside for a moment the effects of juxtaposing Gregor's pathetic death with the family's comic rebirth: that issue is crucial and needs its own frame of reference. But we need only to consider the amusing way in which Kafka describes the family's triumph in order to realize how artful the artless psychology becomes in the telling. When the boarders enter in the morning, they are still arrogant, but as they stand looking at Gregor's corpse, they put their hands in the pockets of their somewhat shabby coats ("etwas abgenützten Röckchen"). Their shabbiness, of which we had no indication before and which might remind us of Mr. Samsa's stained, used messenger's coat, becomes apparent with Gregor's death and announces the imminent defeat of the powers of intimidation. At this moment, as if on cue, the Samsas emerge from the parents' bedroom, the father walking in the middle in his uniform, the two women flanking him, their arms linked with his. Now that there is no more son to complicate the father's possession of the women and no more symbol of the family's unworthiness, this united primal horde advances directly upon the middle lodger, whom the father orders from the house. Confronting each other like mirror images, triad faces triad in mock-heroic battle (each with its champion) over the corpse of yesterday's battle. The middle boarder submits and leaves humbly; the other boarders hurry after their fallen leader. Actually those two ridiculous figures hop away ("hüpften"); and, because they had been standing by, rubbing their hands behind their backs, they seem to have acquired their own insectlike mannerisms. If one cares to turn entomological, one might suggest that this hopping and dorsal rubbing of limbs suggest not the sacred and excremental dung beetle, to which the charwoman and Vladimir Nabokov liken Gregor, but the locust. Yet if one wishes to think of plagues and Pharoahs and patriarchs (again, some twenty-five years before *Moses and Monotheism*), one must also remember the comic tone of the description; if any such allusions are present, they lighten as well as deepen the text.

Feeling a burden lifted, the Samsas decide to celebrate by taking a day off from work, first writing excuses to their employers. How wonderfully important and trivial this gesture is. They assert the freedom and rebellion that Gregor had never asserted in his five years as dutiful salesman; they play hooky. The women are still discomforted by the coarse charwoman who wants to tell them boisterously how she got rid of the dead bug, and Mr. Samsa is again irritated by the upright feather in the aggressive woman's hat (apparently the phallic father still resents competition), but they decide to fire that reminder of their past. So, they take a trolley ride into the country, in the warm sunshine, where they realize that their jobs are really advantageous and their prospects good. Noticing that their daughter has blossomed ("aufgeblüht") into a beautiful young girl, the parents think it soon time to find her a husband (no magazine pin-ups for her), and she seems to respond by stretching her young body in a new beginning. Furthermore, this happens at the end of March, which is surely not the cruelest month for this family, whose rebirth happens suddenly and fairly painlessly.

There has been much disagreement about this ending: in fact, Kafka himself was not satisfied with it. Should we see it as a triumphant assertion of health and happiness, or as the family's obtuse assertion of bourgeois values without their realizing what higher values might have been learned from their drama, or as something more ambivalent? First of all, we must assume that the final description of the family does imply a desirable state. The biographical evidence, including Max Brod's testimonies and the letters to Felice at this time (before the painful vacillations over marriage had begun), indicates that, despite any fears and misgivings, Kafka considered marriage and family life to be a great achievement, one that he later claimed had been denied by his father. Furthermore, the weight of almost the entire story supports this assumption. One must not make too much—although I shall make much—of a bit of violin music or of external parallels between Gregor as a verminous recluse and Kafka as a solitary writer. It is too clever by far to make brief scenes or general analogies determine the entire story, to find keys that open hidden doors, which, when entered, show us the mirror image of the tale, making all ironic and reversing apparent values. Still, the entire presentation of the Samsas' triumph and rebirth must give us more than pause.

Their problems become so narrowly focused, their triumph so swift, and their reversal so apparently complete. Also, the psychological symbolism by which these terms are figured is too pat, too schematic, even to the point of caricature. The methods of presentation become an ironic commentary on the Samsas' development.

Despite the psychological caricatures in sections 1 and 2, the representations of Gregor's condition are complex, illusive, and puzzling: the anthropomorphic image of the inner life is not adequate. Yet in section 3, when the Freudian pattern is transferred to the other Samsas, who replace Gregor in the world, the psychoanalytic theory is quite adequate to the situation. Indeed, if the desires, fears, and conflicts of the inner world could be reduced to the terms in which they are expressed in the Samsas' case, then they might be grasped and governed by the simple gestures whereby Grete rejects the monster and Mr. Samsa kicks out the boarders. If, that is, they could be so reduced; if one could become as naive as the Samsas. But their problems are not Gregor's: they have not been changed into a monstrous vermin, either literally or symbolically. They have shallower problems to confront, comprehend, and solve—at least the problems are shallower as they are presented by the detached narrator and perceived by the characters. Perhaps the Samsas' ability to see their condition so simply—or their inability to see it more complexly—enables them to change that condition, to formulate it in manageable terms and then to take care of it. The authorial perspective is quite complex and subtle in its admiration for, and condescension to, the naiveté of this middle-class family.

This perspective is clarified by a brilliant parable that Kafka wrote in his octavo notebooks on October 23, 1917; he called it "Das Schweigen der Sirenen" ["The Silence of the Sirens"], and began it with the statement, "Beweis dessen, dass auch unzulängliche, ja kindische Mittel zur Rettung dienen können" ["Evidence that even inadequate, indeed childish means may serve to save one"] ("Hochzeitsvorbereitungen"). He explains that the fatal song of the sirens could not be withstood by Odysseus' simple devices of wax to plug the ears and chains to secure himself to the ship's mast; the song could penetrate anything, and the passion in the hearer would snap chains and mast. But even more terrible is the silence of the Sirens from which nothing could ever escape. Attempting to resist the singing with his little stratagems, Odysseus sailed toward the Sirens in innocent delight, and they, seeing the reflected glory in his eyes as he thought confidently of his wax and chains, stood aghast, unsinging, their mouths agape. Odysseus, thinking that they had sung and that he had outwitted them, did not hear their silence and so sailed on as they stared in longing. (Kafka adds in a cunning afterthought that the wily Odysseus may have noticed that the Sirens were silent and may have confounded them and the gods with a trick. But he says that this possibility is beyond comprehension by the mind of man. It surely is beyond the minds of the Samsas, who seem truly naive, not wily.) So the Samsas with their wax and chains, their inadequate, childish means, their family bug and boarders, confound the Sirens by their simplicity and escape temptations to despair and death. In doing so they are not even aware of the most terrible weapon, the silence of the sirens. But Gregor does not have their little stratagems; he hears the song, and perhaps at the last the silence.

After Gregor has been defeated by his father and has seen his mother embrace the victorious father in an all-out Oedipal scenario, he progressively withdraws from such conflicts, carrying with him the festering wound that is both a literal and symbolic cause of his withdrawal. As the Samsas assume the psychological burden of worry, labor, and shame, Gregor loses it. At first he waits hours for the door to be opened onto the living room where the others sit in the evening; he worries about them and sometimes thinks that he ought to take charge of their affairs as he once had done. But in time, with neglect and weakness, he loses his concern and often does not even heed the open door. Many of the traits that had given specific psychological significance to his metamorphosis disappear: his ravenous hunger, his pleasure in acrobatic crawling, his repressed feelings of aggression. He even becomes indifferent to his filth, no longer feeling the guilt or shame that was associated with his metamorphosis.

It is fully appropriate that the scene that takes Gregor most beyond Freudian concerns and then returns him to them for a last flicker should involve the Samsas, the three boarders, and the living room into which Gregor emerges for a third time. Having realized that he was hungry but not for such food as the boarders are glutting themselves with, Gregor hears his sister's violin playing, finds it beautiful for the first time, and thinks that he is finding the way to the unknown nourishment he craves ("der ersehnten unbekannten Nahrung"). Whatever religious, mystical, or aesthetic significance we might find in this music and Gregor's response to it, we can be sure that the significance is not Freudian; that unknown nourishment is not made by a mother's breast, and it is not desired by a pleasure-seeking id. It is beyond not only the pleasure principle, but the Freudian principles as well. Yet, in horrible irony, this music of whatever remote spheres draws Gregor into the family's living room, that psychological arena that he has come to ignore. As he approaches Grete, entering further into the room, his attention slips from the music to the musician to the sister whom he will keep in his room as his own and finally to the girl whose bare neck he will kiss. Within a few sentences Gregor slides down the scale from spiritual quester to the monster guarding the hidden lady to lewd vermin. And as he is again drawn into the psychological scheme, we are again confronted with the contrast between symbolic meaning and grotesque fact. Psychologically we have Gregor's lapse into erotic, incestuous desire. We might even be tempted to recall something Kafka jotted in his diary two months before he wrote *Die Verwandlung*: "Liebe zwischen Bruder und Schwester — die Wiederholung der Liebe zwischen Mutter und Vater" ["Love between brother and sister — the repeating of the love between mother and father"] (*Tagebücher*). And we might note that the image of Gregor guarding his bedroom door in which his sister is hidden repeats the image in section 2 of Gregor pressed against that door, which then separated his mother from his father. But we also must contend with the literal image of the vermin pressing its jaws against the girl's soft neck. Here again is the jarring double perspective: the human character whose impulses we can explain so well and the creature whose appearance mocks our explanations with a revulsion that no theory can dispel.

It is appropriate for the psychological perspective that precisely at this point in the story the middle boarder calls out and points at Gregor, first in scorn, then in anger. Having reentered the Samsas' room and experienced forbidden erotic longings, Gregor automatically calls forth the accuser that has been judging the Samsas. After the sister then disowns the creature, another psychological defeat to another incestuous assertion, Gregor returns to his room where he dies, thus ending the long decline that began when his father had injured him during the last emergence.

As Gregor lies in the darkness of his locked room, unable to move, he seems mentally remote from the verminous body to which he had once accustomed himself: "kam es ihm unnatürlich vor, dass er sich bis jetzt tatsächlich mit diesen dünnen Beinchen hatte fortbewegen können" ("It seemed unnatural to him that he should ever actually have been able to move on these feeble little legs"] (*The Complete Stories*). And as he dies we are given no more reminders of his verminous body or of anything suggesting psychological symbolism:

An seine Familie dachte er mit Rührung und Liebe zurück. Seine Meinung darüber, dass er verschwinden müsse, war womöglich noch entschiedener als die seiner Schwester. In diesem Zustand leeren und friedlichen Nachdenkens blieb er, bis die Turmuhr die dritte Morgenstunde schlug. Den Anfang des allgemeinen Hellerwerdens draussen vor dem Fenster erlebte er noch. Dann sank sein Kopf ohne seinen Willen gänzlich nieder, und aus seinen Nüstern strömte sein letzter Atem schwach hervor.

[He thought of his family with tenderness and love. The decision
that he must disappear was one that he held to even more strongly
than his sister, if that were possible. In this state of vacant and
peaceful meditation he remained until the tower clock struck three
in the morning. The first broadening of light in the world outside the window entered his consciousness once more. Then his
head sank to the floor of its own accord and from his nostrils
came the last faint flicker of his breath.]

(*The Complete Stories*)

Gregor dies here not as a monstrous vermin (do bugs have nostrils through
which a dying breath passes?) and not as an Oedipal son (that tenderness
and love are not erotic), but as a human being with affection, acceptance,
and peace. The scene is moving in its quiet, understated gentleness, and we
should not obscure its emotional effects with talk of religious symbolism or
claims that, in thinking of his family, Gregor has slipped back into his old
preoccupations. The morning light is quite effective without being a beatific
radiance, and the love that Gregor feels is hardly the same as his former feelings of duty, responsibility, and possessiveness. The tone of the passage denies
such abstract equations.

Indeed, we should not try to explain the account of Gregor's death
in terms of mysticism, religious allegory (no Christ images, please), or
psychological theory (no death wishes either). It should abide our questions,
as death often does in Kafka's works. By recognizing its lyrical beauty, its
lack of irony or symbols, we can see how strongly it contrasts both with
the broad naturalistic humor that enters immediately afterwards with the
charwoman and with the intellectual humor that follows in the confrontation between the Samsas and the boarders. Gregor's death, to a large extent
the culmination of his increasing withdrawal throughout most of section 3,
is accessible neither to gruff common sense nor to abstract explanations, both
of which project their anthropomorphic images onto a state that recedes into
stubborn silence.

In sum, then, *Die Verwandlung* has a forked structure. In the first two
sections Gregor dominates, representing psychological themes but also acting out incongruities and parodies that question the adequacy of those themes.
In section 3 the story splits, and our attention moves back and forth between
complementary sets of characters. The Samsas, having received Gregor's duties
and frustrations, also receive his Freudian themes, but in such an apparently
unchallenged way that the themes adequately explain the Samsas' condition
and provide pat, somewhat comic solutions. Gregor, by contrast, withdraws
more and more from his "human" concerns of father, mother, prohibitions,

and pleasures: thus he is separated from the Freudian themes that an anthropomorphic psychology describes as the content of the inner world. Only at the eleventh hour does Gregor temporarily join his family in its "human" psychological world, and that brief scene emphasizes how far he has withdrawn and how futile it is for him to look back; it enables him to complete his withdrawal into a quiet, mysterious death through which he enters a realm of pure parable, leaving the Samsas to live in daily life, to struggle with and overcome the cares of everyday.

These last contrasts come from one of Kafka's writings, "Von den Gleichnissen" ["On Parables"], which can furnish a final commentary on the ending of the story and on the relationship between the reader and the entire work:

> Viele beklagen sich, dass die Worte der Weisen immer wieder nur Gleichnisse seien, aber unverwendbar im täglichen Leben, und nur dieses allein haben wir. Wenn der Weise sagt: "Gehe hinüber," so meint er nicht, dass man auf die andere Seite hinübergehen solle, was man immerhin noch leisten könnte, wenn das Ergebnis des Weges wert wäre, sondern er meint irgendein sagenhaftes Drüben, etwas, das wir nicht kennen, das auch von ihm nicht näher zu bezeichnen ist und das uns also hier gar nichts helfen kann. Alle diese Gleichnisse wollen eigentlich nur sagen, dass das Unfassbare unfassbar ist, und das haben wir gewusst. Aber das, womit wir uns jeden Tag abmühen, sind andere Dinge.
> Darauf sagte einer: "Warum wehrt ihr euch? Würdet ihr den Gleichnissen folgen, dann wäret ihr selbst Gleichnisse geworden und damit schon der täglichen Mühe frei."
> Ein anderer sagte: "Ich wette, dass auch das ein Gleichnis ist."
> Der erste sagte: "Du hast gewonnen."
> Der zweite sagte: "Aber leider nur im Gleichnis."
> Der erste sagte: "Nein, in Wirklichkeit; im Gleichnis hast du verloren."

> [Many complain that the words of the wise are always merely parables and of no use in daily life, which is the only life we have. When the sage says: "Go over," he does not mean that we should cross to some actual place, which we could do anyhow if the labor were worth it; he means some fabulous yonder, something unknown to us, something that he cannot designate more precisely either, and therefore cannot help us here in the very least. All these parables really set out to say merely that the incomprehen-

sible is incomprehensible, and we know that already. But the cares
we have to struggle with every day: that is a different matter.

Concerning this a man once said: Why such reluctance? If you
only followed the parables you yourselves would become parables
and with that rid of all your daily cares.

Another said: I bet that is also a parable.

The first said: You have won.

The second said: But unfortunately only in parable.

The first said: No, in reality: in parable you have lost.]

(The Complete Stories)

The first two paragraphs of this extraordinary passage describe Gregor's prog-
ress in the story as he goes over to some fabulous yonder, becomes parables,
and loses his daily cares; whether it is a yonder to which a wise man would
bid one go is a matter of much critical dispute and will have to be settled
by a wiser man than I. The dialogue in the passage then distinguishes between
parable, which is incomprehensible even though it might be experienced (like
the inner world), and interpretation, which is valid only in the everyday world,
the world that is comprehensible because we accept its limits, its categories
and conventions. ("Ich wette, dass auch das ein Gleichnis ist" ["I bet that
is also a parable"] is, in fact, an instance of genre criticism; the second speaker
may have studied at Toronto.) Interpretation accommodates parable to life,
perhaps making it useful ("Du hast gewonnen") ["You have won"], but it
cannot completely describe it, for interpretation is reductive ("im Gleichnis
hast du verloren" ["in parable you have lost"]). Within *Die Verwandlung* Kafka
dramatizes a contrast similar to that described above: Gregor's metamorphosis
is a form of parable; in section 3 the Samsa family acts out an interpretation
of that parable, both clarifying and reducing it in the world of everyday.
In that world they win, both in the validity of their interpretation (psychology
always has correct results) and in its practical consequences. In parable, of
course, they have lost. Correspondingly, the reader is encouraged to interpret the metamorphosis psychologically, although with far more intellectual
understanding than the Samsas, who merely dramatize an interpretation they
could not express. Perhaps the reader may also win in the world as he reduces
a disturbing and frustratingly elusive story to a manageable pattern, an anthropomorphic form. Of course, he too loses in parable.

But Kafka, whose autobiographical accounts show how much he wrestled
with the experiences he represented, had such sensitivity and intelligence that
he could not accept these interpretations of man, of the inner world, as adequate; yet he had enough honesty to admire those who did not see life as

mysterious, who could see it in their own terms and so, like Odysseus, still live. Milena Jesenská explains as much in a letter written in 1920 to Max Brod, who quotes it in his biography of Kafka:

> Gewiss steht die Sache so, dass wir alle dem Augenschein nach fähig sind zu leben, weil wir irgendeinmal zur Lüge geflohen sind, zur Blindheit, zur Begeisterung, zum Optimismus, zu einer Überzeugung, zum Pessimismus oder zu sonst etwas. Aber er ist nie in ein schützendes Asyl geflohen, in keines. Er ist absolut unfähig zu lügen, so wie er unfähig ist, sich zu betrinken. . . . Es gibt sehr gescheite Menschen, die auch keine Kompromisse machen wollen. Aber sie legen Wunderbrillen an, mit denen sie alles anders sehen. Darum brauchen sie keine Kompromisse. Dann können sie rasch Maschine schreiben und Weiber haben. Er steht neben ihnen und schaut sie verwundert an, alles, auch diese Schreibmaschine und diese Weiber. Nie wird er es begreifen.

> [There are very intelligent people who also do not wish to make any compromises. But these put on rose-colored glasses and see everything in a different light. For that reason they do not need to make compromises. For that reason they can type rapidly and have women. He stands beside them and looks at them in astonishment, looks at everything, including the typewriter and the women, in equal amazement. He will never understand it. . . . For, obviously, we are capable of living because at some time or other we took refuge in lies, in blindness, in enthusiasm, in optimism, in some conviction or others, in pessimism or something of that sort. But he has never escaped to any such sheltering refuge, none at all. He is absolutely incapable of living, just as he is incapable of getting drunk.]

> (Max Brod, *Franz Kafka: A Biography*, translated by
> G. Humphreys Roberts and Richard Winston)

How impressive that this man could incorporate into his fiction the demands of mystery and terror and the promises of refuge, and that he could do it so well that readers still argue the relative demands of each. But the squirming fiction exceeds the squamous mind. As we interpret *Die Verwandlung* (and as readers we must, to some extent), we should remember that, no matter how flexible and comprehensive we are, we shall lose in parable. We can hope to win more completely, more interestingly, only in life.

The Impersonal Narrator of *The Metamorphosis*

Roy Pascal

For his second story, *The Metamorphosis* (*Die Verwandlung*), Kafka adopted the same nonpersonal narrator [as in "The Judgment" ("Das Urteil")], and its first sentence proclaims the subordination of the narrator to the chief character. "When Gregor Samsa awoke one morning out of restless dreams he found himself in his bed transformed into a monstrous bug." From this moment the narrator identifies himself almost completely with Gregor, sees and hears through his eyes and ears, and accepts the truth of his metamorphosis as the victim himself must. Except in the coda of the last few pages, describing the revival of the family after the death of Gregor, almost everything we know is passed on to us via the consciousness of Gregor. To his thoughts we have direct access, the others we know as Gregor sees them through the open door and overhears their conversation. His thoughts and impressions are sometimes reported by the narrator much like his spoken words, in inverted commas introduced by such verbs as "thought." But they also invade many passages which, while seeming to express a narrator's view, betray the personal source by a characteristic word here or there. For instance, in the first paragraph, the last sentence might be read as a narrator's comment: "His many — in relationship to his bulk pitifully thin — legs waved helplessly before his eyes." But the preceding sentences have described what Gregor could see of his body when he raised his head, and we are meant to feel the "pitifully" is *his* thought as much as the "waved" applies to *his* vision.

The text continues:

"What has happened to me?" he thought. It was no dream.

From *Kafka's Narrators: A Study of His Stories and Sketches.* © 1982 by Cambridge University Press.

> His room, a proper human room—albeit a little too small—lay
> calmly between its four familiar walls. Above the table on which
> a collection of materials had been spread out—Samsa was a com-
> mercial traveller—hung the picture which he had recently cut out
> of an illustrated magazine and mounted in a pretty gilt frame.

The first sentence in inverted commas seems to distinguish Gregor's thoughts
from the "facts" the narrator lists. But this distinction does not hold. "It
was no dream" is evidently a conclusion of Gregor's, not the narrator's, since
the normal appearance of his room proves it. Not merely "calmly" has meaning
only if thought by Gregor, also the odd phrase, "a human room—albeit a
little too small," critical and reassuring together, has meaning only if it is
a rumination of Gregor's, showing the mean, carping spirit in his smugness.
Other items in the room, his samples and the picture, are mentioned as his
eyes travel to them, and again the expression "pretty gilt frame" with its
smugness has meaning only if it belongs to him and not the narrator. But,
on the other hand, the parenthesis "Samsa was a commercial traveller" is
an explanatory communication from narrator to reader.

This narratorial passage is followed by Gregor's resentful reflexions on
his unsatisfactory profession and his superiors, given in direct speech; a long
passage of free indirect speech, peppered with exclamatory questions and
characteristic phrases (as when the porter is called "the boss's minion, a creature
with no backbone or mind of his own"); narratorial descriptions of his behaviour as he tries to get out of bed, listens to what his family is doing or saying
when the chief clerk (*Prokurist*) arrives etc.; and reproductions of the discus-
sions Gregor hears, and takes part in, given in direct speech. None of these
methods provides problems of interpretation except the narratorial descrip-
tive form, which consistently betrays that ambiguity we have already observed
in the opening two paragraphs. That is: while the narrator's standpoint is
determined by the consciousness and concern of the character Gregor and
he usually is concerned only to make Gregor's feelings and intentions evident, he also sometimes demonstrates a more independent purpose and indeed
offers the reader the chance of becoming the objective observer he emphatically does become in the final pages, after Gregor's death. It is this narratorial stance that requires a closer examination, the object of which can
be formulated thus: why, if the supreme function of the narrator is to communicate to the reader the chief character's view and judgment and his world,
without the corrective of an authoritative evaluation, does this narrator still
retain some independence of function? This independence appears in several
forms.

The chief form is as a technical aid to the narrative. This we have already seen when the parenthesis "Samsa was a commercial traveller" enables us to understand why Gregor's eye lights on certain objects in his room. There are many such bits of helpful information that the narrator smuggles in, as if, when we are looking at a detective film, a neighbour who has already seen it whispers to us what we should look out for. In this way we are told that the Samsa's maid keeps to the kitchen and locks the door, we receive a precise description of the elaborate meal that Gregor's sister puts out for him, and brief character-sketches of the new charwoman and the trio of lodgers. It is true that often there are suggestions that these facts are present to Gregor's consciousness, as when the information that all three lodgers have beards is, as it were, validated by the statement "as Gregor once noticed through the crack of the door," but it is clear that our information often comes from some other source than Gregor. I do not think these occasional bits of supplementary information weaken in any way the intensity of the narrative, since they do not offer an alternative view or evaluation.

It is different with one such addition. The scene when Gregor intrudes into the family room, in which his sister is playing to the lodgers, is in all essentials described from his point of view, perhaps with a few enlargements to compensate for the limitations imposed on his vision. But as he creeps into the full sight of the lodgers and the family and creates panic among them, we are told of the filthy state he is in, with "threads, hair, remains of food" clinging to his back. For a moment we see him as the others see him, in a state he is unconscious of (normally he is only too aware of his disgusting appearance). This constitutes a change of perspective that is different from the others mentioned, since it means a switch from the main character's consciousness to that of other characters, and though it is only a momentary effect, I find it disconcerting. That we feel it as a dislocation must be due to the depth of our normal absorption in the perspective of the chief character. For, from the first sentence, it is Gregor himself who sees himself changed into a loathsome bug, while the others (including the narrator) only confirm what he feels and asserts. It is only under this condition that the story—fairy tale or parable—is presented to us.

There are also other ways in which the narrator's hand is evident, especially when the story is temporarily released from the account of concrete events as they occur in Gregor's presence. Occasionally the narrator summarises a process, telling us for instance "In this way Gregor was given his food every day" or "Gregor spent the days and nights with almost no sleep." The long account of his labours for his family and his hopes to retrieve his father's business failure and provide for the education of his sister is expressly stated to represent the "utterly useless thoughts" running through his head while he listens to the family discussion, but the succinct narratorial account here again puts the reader at a distance from the situation, frees him from the immediacy of the tale, gives him the relief of an intellectual grasp of the situation. The most striking passage of this kind is the opening of the third section of the story. Here the narrator sums up the change in the father's attitude to Gregor during the month that followed his father's furious attack on him. Now, we are told, the father seemed to have decided to treat him as a member of the family, not an enemy; and we understand that Gregor gathers this from various bits of evidence available through the open sitting-room door. We can even hear a typical bit of complex free indirect speech in the last words of this paragraph, that "family duty commanded that one swallowed one's disgust and suffered, accepted and suffered," for it is Gregor's thought quoting unmistakeably the overheard words of his father. Here again, though we cannot speak of a different perspectival angle in these words, since their source is as ever the character Gregor Samsa, there is the difference of distance, a distance in this case peculiar to story-making, a long temporal focus replacing the near focus and thus inducing a relaxation of the almost unbearable tension of the story. For this tension arises not simply from the horror of the events but above all from our inescapable immersion in them through the nature of the narrative perspective.

Such pauses in the movement of a narrative are very common in traditional novels and function as a temporary relaxation of tension — Cervantes makes fun of them when he closes a chapter at the moment when Don Quixote's sword is about to cleave his antagonist's head (bk. 1, chap. 8). They belong naturally to a type of narrative structure in which the intrusive authoritative narrator has many such tricks at his disposal. But, while in *The Metamorphosis* such changes in the temporal or spatial perspective are few and slight, they achieve a relaxation of a different type, one that affects not the tension of a dramatic event but the whole oppressive spell the reader submits to as a result of the narrative perspective. These slight pauses are indeed anticipations of the change that occurs after Gregor's death, when the family revives, decently rejoicing in its liberation from the son who, while he was their chief support, had because of this drained them of responsibility and confidence. The reader too, now freed from the mediation of Gregor, has direct access to their thoughts and feelings, even to those of the charwoman. So that this coda seems in fact to be outside the magic circle of the story. Kafka twice expressed his distaste for this "unreadable ending," but gave no hint of the grounds for his dissatisfaction.

Different readers will feel these variations in the narrative perspective with different intensity. But all would agree that, if there is any inconsistency in the structure, it impairs hardly at all the power of the work. If we have in part answered the questions posed above, we have still to face the most important, underlying question: why does Kafka employ in these tales an impersonal narrator, if his essential function is only to communicate the chief character's view? Why should he not have written a first-person story and avoided the lapses that have been pointed out? The question has relevance in regard to other Kafka stories too, and in particular to the novels.

In the first place, the use of such a narrator is a great technical convenience, since it makes it possible to establish a physical scene or sum up a long process with greater clarity and economy than if the author is closely bound to the consciousness of the character. Though the narrator stands beside the character and remains true to his perspective, he can select and order the objects or events in the character's experience in order to make the appropriate impact on the reader. Every character, like every living person, registers his outer and inner experience with differing grades of awareness, and at any particular moment will not always be able to distinguish the significant from the trivial; the narrator can so differentiate and by various means can subtly make the reader aware of a line of significance within a chaos of contingency—as for instance he does at the opening of the story, when Gregor responds to his appalling transformation with the apparently ludicrously irrelevant and trivial resentment directed at his employers.

Of course, in stories of the type of "The Judgment" and *The Metamorphosis*, in which the chief character dies, an external narrator is particularly useful, not simply because the character cannot describe his own death and its results, but also because it is hard to find for a dead man the perspective in which he would see his past life. There are in fact stories written in the first person in which this person dies, but the endings always seem awkward and contrived. We shall find that in his later stories Kafka repeatedly prefers a first-person narrative, but for stories which describe a continuing situation which lacks a conclusive ending.

The interpretative function of the objective impersonal narrator in both these early Kafka stories is, above all, the provision of a guarantee for the events recounted, a guarantee of a special kind. The objective voice seems to confirm the character's situation through an impersonal affirmation and a slightly different focus, slightly further away from things than the character himself. We can detect its general effect in that startling first sentence of *The Metamorphosis*: "When Gregor Samsa awoke one morning out of restless

dreams he found himself in his bed transformed into a monstrous bug."
Though we later discover that this statement corresponds to Gregor's own
conviction, it is in its form deliberately and emphatically an objective narratorial
assertion and this fact should not be wiped out of the reader's consciousness.
We hear in it the objective voice of fiction, the invitation to enter the world
of imagination and to suspend disbelief. Because of the authoritative nature
of this narratorial voice, that makes itself heard from time to time later in
the story, we are warned against taking the story as the mere account of
a character's hallucination or as a study in psychopathology. But what guarantee
does this voice give? This calm constatation of a fantastic monstrosity is
clearly not intended to persuade us that it and the following events belong
to the normal order of reality, however realistic, psychologically and physically,
their description may be. How then do we read it? I believe as a folk tale
or parable in which, if we are presented with unrealistic fantasies, we know that
we are not thereby invited to take them as real in an ordinary sense but urged
to look into them for some meaning, some illumination on life that they
will provide through their impact upon the circumstances into which they
burst. The guarantee of the impersonal narrator is a guarantee of meaning;
he asks us to accept the presupposition of Gregor's metamorphosis in order
(as we find out) to enquire into the relations of son and father, son and family,
and especially the power-rivalries involved—in the same way as in Kafka's
novels, *The Trial* and *The Castle*, we are not to question the reality and
authority of the law courts or the castle but to experience the meaning they
have for the characters who seek admittance. This is a typical feature of Kafka's
storytelling that . . . forces the reader to look beyond the surface network
of the story for another, symbolic meaning.

But if we now consider together these various items that the impersonal
narrator contributes to *The Metamorphosis*, we find this contribution is of
greater significance than we earlier suspected. For, taken together, they
establish the structure of a story—not only are the scenes filled out by pieces
of narratorial information, but the narrator opens and closes the story, sets
the scenes, establishes them as phases of a story for which he also determines
the movement in time, allowing us sometimes to be absorbed in the moment,
sometimes from a longer focus to view the passage of days. In *The Metamorphosis*, as could be observed in "The Judgment," the narrator's adoption
of the main character's perspective makes the reader experience the events
as if they were present, especially in the sense that they have the incoherence
of the present and do not point to an outcome. But this presentness of
experience is conveyed through the past tense, the narrative preterite, with
which both stories open and continue. And, from the beginning of each story,

this past tense proclaims that we are to read events that make up a completed whole, that is told, as it were, in retrospect. Because of this, the story can be articulated in its structure, have its phases that lead to its outcome. Thus a double process take place in the reader. On the one hand he is immersed in the experience of the main character, cut off from an alternative source and alternative evaluations; but on the other hand he is directed by the structure of the story, which is cunningly devised both to provide an intense participation in the character's experience but also to establish it as forming a whole with a peculiar coherence. In this way the Kafka narrator provides therefore not only for experience but also for understanding; for understanding is the *raison d'être* of storytelling, even if the understanding implied is not what we usually expect by the term. [Elsewhere] I have suggested the relevance of that strange abstract form that Kafka called Odradek: "The whole seems meaningless, it is true, but is in its peculiar way complete." The "meaning" Kafka refers to here is not any allegorical message, but more simply the use or function of the various parts of the figure, their relationship to one another, their coherence. It is the same with these stories. The reader is at first troubled to grasp the psychological coherence of the various parts, the connexion of event and mental response, of purpose and behaviour, of words and thoughts. But the story structure, its completedness, forces us to seek this coherence, to discover relationships between thoughts and situations, the coherence of this apparent incoherence, to accept in fact a coherence that is startingly different from that which the conventional story has lived by.

We cannot evade the question of the style and in particular the question, what contribution does the narrative stance and structure make to the meaning of "The Judgment" and *The Metamorphosis*? I will try to answer this question within the wider framework of the modern novel.

The general trend in the modern novel to integrate the fictitious narrator into the imaginative structure, to reduce the identity and function of this once near-omniscient and obtrusive authority to that of privileged insight and imaginative empathy, takes different forms in the work of James Joyce, Virginia Woolf, William Faulkner, Alfred Döblin, Jean-Paul Sartre and others. In these early stories of Kafka we can recognise this trend, though in a highly characteristic, peculiar form. In fact Kafka's form emerges so naturally out of the imagined situation and seems to be so lacking in theoretical intention that for a long time he was looked on as an odd-man-out, and I believe that the first imaginative writer to recognise the representative and theoretical significance of his narrative perspective was Sartre in *Qu'est-ce que la littérature* and, after Sartre, Robbe-Grillet.

In these two stories the narrator has been divested of most of his traditional powers: he is not an independent authority, can offer no significant objective information and no independent explanations, whether material or psychological, cannot present scenes or events from an angle of vision substantially different from that of the chief character, and cannot provide the reader with authoritative moral judgments or norms. He offers no grounds for an explicit interpretation. One is tempted to say that all this narrator — or rather this narrative function, since the narrating medium has no personal identity — can do is to immerse us in the experience of the chief character, and this certainly seems to be the most marked aspect of our reading experience. Characteristically it means immersion in the present situation of the character, in the stream of events and thoughts along which we are borne in their ambiguity and uncertainty of direction and meaning, without foreknowledge or presentiment of the outcome, the future. The past of the characters we know essentially only through the thoughts and memories of the chief characters which give anything but an unbiased, undistorted, authoritative view. Thus, when the ending comes, it has not the traditional enlightening, fulfilling function of an ending, for it does not resolve puzzles and problems. it does not relieve the distress of the story, but seems only a reaffirmation of the arbitrary doom that has weighed on the character from the first. We are tempted to feel the title "The Judgment" to be a supreme irony, for is this sentence that Georg accepts and executes a judgment in *our* eyes? The narrator does not let us know whether he acknowledges it as such, and I believe critics are on the wrong tack when they seek some moral or other formula that would demonstrate the justice of this sentence and thus assuage its harshness — as they also are when they propose moral justifications of Gregor Samsa's fate.

This narrator is a wonderfully apt instrument for these stories, as he is for the novels. In both these early stories the chief character is hemmed in and crippled, spiritually distorted by his relationship with family and father. His fitful activity only spins him more inextricably in a web of love and hate, dependence and power, selflessness and egoism; half paralysed, he is unable to break out into independence and capable only of suffering; his tormented thoughts only intensify his suffering and impotence. That there is here no independent narratorial voice, viewpoint, judgment, is of profound significance, since we are faced with a fateful situation which defies any objective judgment, blame, or apportionment of responsibility. The fact that this narrator is absorbed in the hero is what creates that intense enclosedness of Kafka's stories. There is no escape from the spell they weave, scarcely an opportunity for reflexion, contemplation, for a relaxation of tension, until the spell is broken by the death of the narrator's chief medium, the chief character. And at that point the reader looks back in almost uncomprehending horror, cut off from this strange experience as the awakened sleeper is cut off from his nightmare.

But, if this is the dominant experience of the reader, that he feels most consciously and keenly, it is not the whole truth and needs qualifications here and there. In these stories we are not imprisoned in the unrelaxing obsession and suffering of the chief character as we are for instance in Dostoevsky's *Notes from the Underground*, in which the only medium is the character himself. I have pointed out the many ways in which an independent narrator does appear, not as a person or judge but as an agent in the storytelling. Some of these interventions, as when the narrator inserts some necessary bit of information, are of little significance. But some, though scarcely registered by the reader, are a powerful subliminal influence: those in which a black humour asserts the independent comment of the narrator and especially those through which the narrator sets a new scene, condenses the flow of time, creates phases of the story — for instance the three sections of *The Metamorphosis* and the variations of temporal and physical focus within them. Not only the endings of the stories betray this independent agency, but also the structure of incident, including the striking opening of each story. None of these interventions offers an "explanation" or interpretation of what is occurring. Their significance is that through their form they create meaning in the sense that they create a story-whole in which each part and item has a place, a function. The narrator, however much he identifies himself with the chief character, always also is carrying out this constructive task, placing his hero in a narrative whole. This is nowhere more clearly evident than in the endings, not only since the independent narrator most clearly emerges at this moment, but most significantly since the ending is recognised to be the goal to which the whole of each story is directed and which determines the relationship of the incidents: a goal that is implied by the preterite tense itself, the instrument of retrospective narrative. Television daily gives us clues to the profound significance of the compositional function of endings: the experience of a football match as it takes place is astonishingly different from viewing it after the result is known. Of course, the relationship of the characters in a story to the ending is infinitely more complex and variable than that of players in a competitive game, but in the final analysis it is the ending that holds all together. In the case of the Kafka stories, the sort of coherence and "meaning" that we discover is so puzzlingly unconventional that we should be lost if the story structure and ending did not imperatively require us to seek them.

So there are two contrary impulses in the narratorial stance of these stories—one, the immersion in the present situation of the character, that seems to preclude a knowledge of an outcome, and the other, the subtle assertion of a completed action seen in retrospect. Together they create the story structure even though at times, especially in the endings, the replacement of the first by the second can cause the reader unease. I believe Kafka's own unease over the ending of *The Metamorphosis* (as of "In the Penal Colony") must have been due, at least in part, to this contradiction of form, since we find that he creates in "In the Penal Colony" a different type of ending, one that is inconclusive, open, and in the novels could not bring himself to complete and round off the experience he was communicating. And perhaps this contradiction in narratorial stance is an important element in Kafka's later adoption of a personal narrator writing in the present tense about a noncompleted situation and continuing problem. This is a development I hope to investigate—though of course I am not suggesting that Kafka's development arises from a technical problem. I see it as a struggle to find a medium for his vision or message, a struggle that involved the discovery of an appropriate narrative form.

From Marx to Myth: The Structure and Function of Self-Alienation in Kafka's *Metamorphosis*

Walter H. Sokel

Kafka's uniqueness as a narrative author lies, among other things, in the literalness with which the metaphors buried in linguistic usage come alive and are enacted in the scenes he presents. The punishing machine devised by the Old Commander in *The Penal Colony*, for instance, engraves the law that the condemned have transgressed on their minds by imprinting it literally on their flesh. By the appellation "vermin," linguistic usage designates the lowest form of human self-contempt. Seeing himself as vermin, and being treated as such by his business and family, the travelling salesman Gregor Samsa literally turns into vermin.

Kafka's narratives enact not only the metaphors hidden in ordinary speech, but also ideas crucial in the history of thought. *The Metamorphosis* is a striking example. Gregor Samsa's transformation into vermin presents self-alienation in a literal way, not merely a customary metaphor become fictional fact. The travelling salesman wakes up one morning and cannot recognize himself. Seeing himself as a gigantic specimen of vermin, he finds himself in a fundamental sense estranged from himself. No manner more drastic could illustrate the alienation of a consciousness from its own being than Gregor Samsa's startled and startling awakening.

The idea of human self-alienation has played a crucial role in modern thought from German classical Idealism to Marxism and Existentialism. First encountered in the thought of Wilhelm von Humboldt, Schiller, Fichte, and Hegel, and subsequently in Feuerbach and Marx, this idea always implies the individual's estrangement (*Entfremdung*) from his humanity or "human

From *The Literary Review* 26, no. 4 (Summer 1983). © 1983 by Fairleigh Dickinson University.

species being," i.e., from the individual's membership in the human species. The individual is estranged from himself insofar as he is alienated from his essential nature as a human being.

Rooted as he was in German Idealism and the tradition of German classical literature, the young Marx saw the essential nature of the human species residing in freely productive activity. Human species-being was for him the production of objects that were literally *Gegen-stände*, things that having issued from the labor of his hands and mind now face their producer as the objects of his world. Thus the human species defined by world-creating or world-modifying activity. It is an activity that by virtue of its productive inventiveness humanizes nature. In order to be truly human, this praxis must be, at least partly, self-determined. Work must be engaged in for its own sake. It must have been chosen, partially at least, for its intrinsic pleasure. It must not merely be dictated by external need or the commands of others. In exact analogy to Immanuel Kant's corollary to the categorical imperative, which defines genuine morality, genuinely human labor for Marx must be at least partially its own end, its own freely chosen purpose, and not entirely "a means" for something else such as the satisfaction of extrinsic needs or the insurance of mere survival. To qualify as truly human, labor must always have an element of free choice. It must, at least partly, be its own reward and satisfaction. "At any time" it must "be considered its own purpose, an end in itself."

This freedom of doing one's work for its own sake, for the joy it affords the worker, is the factor that, according to Marx, distinguishes human from animal productivity. Animals, Marx observes, "produce only under the compulsion of physical need. Man, on the other hand, produces even when he is free of physical need, and only in this freedom is he humanly creative. . . . Such production is his active species being. By virtue of it, nature itself appears as man's creation and his reality" (translation mine). Only where work appears as its own reward are human beings truly human. Where it is imposed solely by economic necessity, the worker is not merely alienated from himself as an individual; he is estranged from his humanity. Marx's idea of human self-alienation is not restricted to factory work, but includes any kind of work in which an individual is engaged merely for the wage or income it brings him. The worker is dehumanized wherever his work fails to involve his creative urge and desire.

Here we have arrived at the prehistory of Gregor Samsa's metamorphosis, as the reader learns from Gregor's reminiscences of and meditations about his job as a travelling salesman. We learn that Gregor had been estranged from himself in his all-consuming work even before he finds himself literally estranged from his bodily being. Gregor had found his work unbearable.

He had longed for nothing more passionately than to leave his job, after telling the head of his firm his true opinion of this job. Gregor's profound self-alienation corresponds, with uncanny precision, to Marx's definition of the "externalization" of work under capitalism:

> His work is *external* to the worker, i.e., it does not form part
> of his essential being so that instead of feeling well in his work,
> he feels unhappy, instead of developing his free physical and mental
> energy, he abuses his body and ruins his mind.

Gregor Samsa's professional activity has obviously been such purely instrumental work, external to himself, imposed upon him by the necessity of bailing out his bankrupt family, supporting them, and paying back his parents' debt to the boss of his firm. It is not only joyless and uncreative, it is totally determined by needs external to itself and Gregor. Freedom of creativeness—according to Marx the essence of truly human labor—finds an outlet in Samsa's life, prior to his metamorphosis, only in the carpentry in which he indulges in free evenings. Parenthetically we might recall that Kafka himself hated his bureaucrat's desk job because it served as a mere means to a purpose totally extrinsic to itself, namely a relatively short work day, and found by contrast genuine satisfaction in carpentering and gardening, activities chosen for their own sake, which, like writing, united creativeness with the satisfaction of inner needs.

Compared to accusations of his office work found in his autobiographical documents, Kafka's story, *The Metamorphosis*, "systemizes," as it were, the Marxist factor, not by conscious design, of course, but by virtue of the astonishing parallelism in the point of view, particularly the presentation of self-alienation. Gregor's sole reason for enduring the hated position, the need to pay his parents' "debt" to his boss, drastically highlights the doubly extrinsic purpose of Gregor's work. For not only is his labor alien to his true desires, but its sole purpose, its fruit—the salary or commission that it affords him— does not even belong to him. Gregor's toil does not serve his own existence. It is not his own *Lebensmittel*, to use Marx's term—if left to himself, he would have quit long before—it belongs to and serves another.

This other is Gregor's father. He is the non-working beneficiary and exploiter of Gregor's labor. The product of this labor is the money which Gregor brings home. This money belongs to the other who does not work himself, but enjoys and disposes of the fruits of Gregor's work: "the money which Gregor had brought home every month—he himself had kept only a few pennies to himself—had not been used up completely and had accrued to form a small *capital*" (italics and translations mine). Gregor's father had expropriated the "surplus value" of Gregor's labor and formed with it his — to be sure, very modest — capital." Gregor's relationship to his father thus represents an exact paradigm of the worker's exploitation by his capitalist employer, as described by Marx. The worker is alienated from the product of his labor because he has to yield it to the capitalist. The latter retains the lion's share for himself and returns to the worker only what the latter barely needs to survive. Through this despoiling of the fruits of his work the worker's existence becomes, in the words of Marx, "self-sacrifice and castigation": "In the last analysis, the extrinsic nature of his work is shown to the worker by the fact that his work is not his, but belongs to another. . . . it is the loss of his self." Gregor's metamorphosis literally enacts this "loss of self." It makes drastically visible the self-estrangement that existed even before his metamorphosis.

It is the father's "capital" that leaves Gregor tied to his servitude and bondage, for as the narrator says, "with this *surplus money* [Gregor] could have paid back a much larger part of his father's debt to his boss and the day on which he could have freed himself from this job would have been much closer." (Italics mine).

The last-mentioned fact represents a point at which an entirely different interpretative dimension intersects the Marxist framework of self-alienation that we have so far considered by itself. Although we have by no means as yet exhausted the parallelism between the Marxist concept of self-alienation and the structure and function of Gregor Samsa's metamorphosis in Kafka's text, we might state at this point that Kafka's *The Metamorphosis* is by no means completely defined, if merely seen as the literal enactment of self-alienation. Even if we were to restrict ourselves to this aspect, the centrality of the concept of self-alienation in modern thought would demand additional interpretative frameworks from which to approach Kafka's text, such as psychoanalytic, existentialist, biographical, linguistic, and phenomenological systems of reference which all must needs play important parts in a relatively comprehensive interpretation of Kafka's richly referential narrative.

However, what we shall consider now is Kafka's *The Metamorphosis* as the telling of a myth, for the mythic dimension relates to the Marxist one the way a picture frame relates to the picture which it contains and transcends, at one and the same time. In order to recognize this relationship, we shall have to consider the *mythos* of *The Metamorphosis*. I use the term "mythos" in the Aristotelian sense as the whole chain of fictive events in their chronological as distinct from their narrated order.

The initial point of the mythos is not Gregor's transformation, but the business failure of Gregor's father five years before. This failure led to the contracting of the burdensome debt to the head of Gregor's firm. Thus the mythos begins with a family's cataclysmic fall into adversity through the fault of the father, more precisely the parents, since the text speaks of "die Schuld der Eltern" and only afterward of "die Schuld des Vaters." The German word *Schuld* signifies debt, guilt, and causative fault. This triple meaning is crucial to the understanding of Kafka's mythos. If understood in the sense of debt, the *Schuld* of Gregor's parents belongs to socioeconomic quotidian reality. If understood in the two other senses, *Schuld* belongs to a framework of moral and religious values. The text's repeated use of the singular *Schuld* in contrast to the more customary plural *Schulden* for debt provides a subliminally effective counterpoint to the obvious surface meaning of the word.

This subliminal allusion to guilt receives corroboration from the position of "die Schuld der Eltern" ("the guilt of the parents") at the initial point of the narrative mythos. This position creates a subtle analogy to the fall of mankind as told in Genesis. To be sure, this analogy amounts to the faintest of hints. However, we cannot and must not avoid noting the allusion if we take seriously Kafka's view of language as expressed in one of his aphorisms: "Language can only be used allusively for anything outside the sensory world. (Translation mine).

The son of these guilty parents—Gregor—has to assume their guilt and pay it off "by the sweat of his countenance" (to quote Genesis), by his self-consuming drudgery for his parents' creditor. In the allusive context established by the semantic ambiguity of *Schuld*, Gregor's profoundly alienated existence prior to his metamorphosis establishes the parallel to man's fate after the expulsion from paradise. Like the children of Adam and Eve, Gregor through his sonship in the flesh has been condemned to a perennial debtor's existence. The two semantic realms of *Schuld*—debt and guilt—converge in the fateful consequence of the father's debt. With it, the father surrendered his family to a world in which the exploitation of man by man holds infernal sway. The world to which the father's failing has handed over his family is ruled by the principles of capitalist economics. In this world, the family ceases to be a family in the original and ideal sense of a community in which the bonds of blood—the *Blutkreis* to which Kafka in discussing "The Judgment" accords his highest respect—and natural affection prevail. Instead the family falls victim to the egotistical principle of *gegenseitige Übervorteilung* (mutual defrauding) in which Marx saw the governing principle of human life under capitalism.

Precisely because of his self-sacrifice in assuming his father's debt, Gregor rises to power as the breadwinner in his family and threatens to displace his father as the head of the household. This process reverses itself with Gregor's metamorphosis. Gregor's self-inflicted debasement entails his father's rejuvenation and return to power. These successive displacements — first the father's, then the son's — which find their parallel in Grete's ambiguous liberation through her brother's fall, have their contrastive complements in the parasitic exploitation of the winners by the losers. Before Gregor's metamorphosis, the father was the parasite. After the metamorphosis, the son assumes this role.

A world is shown in which the enjoyment of advantages by the one has to be purchased at the cost of the other. This is the world in a fallen state. Gregor's initial self-sacrifice through work whips up his pride in his ability to support his family in style. Those had been "happy times" when he had been able to "amaze and delight" his family by putting his hard-earned money on their table. But his self-surrender to his work causes a twofold alienation. Inwardly he remains estranged from his work because it is the kind of labor that cannot satisfy a human being. Outwardly his rise to power in the family overshadows the other members and results in their alienation from him. "A special warmth toward him was no longer forthcoming," so the text informs us. Long bedfore his metamorphosis, Gregor and his family have lived coldly and incommunicatively side by side.

The metamorphosis reveals this alienation in its essence as *den völligen Verlust des Menschen* ("the total dehumanization of man") in which Marx saw the ultimate fate of man under capitalism. But it has another and ultimately more important function. Through it Gregor ceases to treat the *Schuld* of his parents as a debt that can be paid back by work, and assumes the *Schuld* in its deeper meaning. He no longer tries to pay back the *Schuld*; he incorporates is. With his incarnation he raises the narrative mythos from its socioeconomic to its mythic meaning.

That Gregor's metamorphosis literally incarnates guilt becomes apparent first of all by the fact that his immediate reaction to his transformation is a guilty conscience. He has missed the hour of his work and feels guilty for it. He feels guilty for having plunged his family into misfortune. He is ashamed. He seeks to hide, to make himself invisible. But even apart from all subjectively felt or morally accountable guilt, guilt becomes evident in him objectively. For his transformation into vermin entails the crassest form of parasitic exploitation, a perfect turning of the tables on his family. His metamorphosis compels them to work for him and in his place. Because of him they will henceforth be "overlooked and overtired," condemned to suffer the fate of "paupers." To be sure, his father's bankruptcy five years before had condemned Gregor to an exploited existence. But by his metamorphosis, Gregor himself turns into an arch exploiter, the archetypal parasite which vermin represents. His very appearance as *ungeheueres Ungeziefer* is emblematic and flaunts a gigantic form of parasitism. Even as Gregor's subsequent daydream of declaring his love to his sister constitutes a gruesome parody of bourgeois-sentimental courtship, so his vermin existence as such embodies exploitation as the essence of human relations. By embodying parasitism in his shape, Gregor objectifies the guilt of his entire society. This guilt had originally shown itself in his father when he secretly cheated his son and furtively put aside his son's earnings to form "a modest capital." Reversing their roles, the son now becomes exploitation in its most honest clearly visible form. To use T. S. Eliot's term, most appropriate to Kafka's tale, Gregor becomes the "objective correlative" of the insight that exploitation is the original guilt of mankind. Gregor literally becomes what his father had committed in stealthily performed acts.

In the narrative mythos of Kafka's tale, the metamorphosis literally takes the place of the father's debt. The text mentions a debt only for the prehistory of *The Metamorphosis*, as a flashback in Gregor's memory. In the action which the reader witnesses, the debt plays no role. The text never mentions it again. It seems that Gregor's *Schreckgestalt*, his new terrifying shape, which the first morning after his awakening had chased away the deputy of the firm, has thereby also cancelled the parents' debt. In place of it, Gregor himself has become "the misfortune" of the Samsa family.

Later, the father wounds Gregor with an apple which rots and festers in Gregor's flesh. This apple functions not only as a renewed allusion to "the guilt of first parents"; it also signifies the function of Gregor's metamorphosis as the literal incorporation of his father's guilt. Gregor, mortally hurt by the blind "rage" of his father, has obviously become his father's victim in the concluding section of the story. Yet this final violation of the son by the father only repeats in a transparent way Gregor's initial victimization. In the beginning, Gregor had to assume his father's debt and thus become its victim. At that time *Schuld* had been understood in the economic and juridical meaning of debt. By his metamorphosis Gregor incorporates this *Schuld* and transforms it from a legal-contractual concept into its full and profound meaning as the concretely visible form of alienated life. Parenthetically one might say that the *Schuld* which the father bequeathes to the son is in the last analysis life itself. The "rotting apple in the flesh" not only causes, but also embodies Gregor's protracted dying. This seems to suggest that the original "guilt of the parents" was the dubious "gift" of physical existence. This reading would connect *The Metamorphosis* with numerous other works by Kafka and with the spirit of his aphorisms.

In contrast to his father, Gregor does not incur guilt; he is guilt. His incarnation of guilt corresponds to Christ's incarnation of God in man, in one sense only. Like Christ, Gregor takes the cross upon himself to erase "the guilt of the parents." But in contrast to Christ, Gregor does not merely assume suffering by his fellow creatures; he also assumes their guilt. Since he has made guilt identical with himself, he must liberate the world, i.e., his family, from himself.

"The guilt of the parents" showed itself as indebtedness. It constituted capitulation to the world in its capitalist makeup. In strict consequence, economic determination inserts itself now into the myth as Kafka presents it. This insertion can be understood in sociocultural and, indeed, Marxist categories. The plot inserted into the mythic events depicts a classic case of the proletarianization of a petty-bourgeois household. The "modest capital" created by the father's exploitation of Gregor's work for the firm "sufficed . . . not at all to permit the family to live on its interest." In consequence the family loses its bourgeois status, its economic independence. Father Samsa remains the omnipotent potentate in his family. But in the world outside, he toils as a humble bank messenger. By the self-elimination of her brother as a human being, Grete rises to monopolistic eminence and privilege in her family. But in the outside world, she has to serve strangers as a poor salesgirl. Gregor's mother is reduced to taking sewing and dressmaking work home. In regard to the socioeconomic world of exploited labor, Gregor, by the horrible paradox that is his metamorphosis, is now the only "free" member of the family, the only one who does not have to labor and let himself be exploited by the world outside.

The family's proletarianization reaches its nadir when it has to yield the control over its household to the three lodgers. According to Marx, as capitalism increasingly absorbs all pre-capitalistic forms of human life, "the contrast between natural and social existence becomes progressively more extreme." In Kafka's tale, the displacement of the "natural," traditional head of the family, the father, by the three strangers exemplifies the development described by Marx. The three lodgers assume the dominant place in the household merely by virtue of their paying power. Kafka's plot mimetically conforms to and expresses Marx's observation of the historic change from blood kinship to money as the determining element in all human relationships. *The Metamorphosis* shows how the basis of power, even within the "natural" unit of the family, slips from blood, age, and sex, the foundations of the father's dominance, to money which makes the unrelated strangers the rulers of the family. The family forfeits its autonomy even within its own walls. Of course, even prior to this loss, the family's independence had been [in] appearance only since the father's debt to Gregor's firm had handed it over to the tyranny of the business world, represented by the creditor's firm. The lodgers' invasion of the household and their assumption of absolute control over it thus, in Marx's words, only "brings to a head" what had been inherent in the family's enslavement to the capitalist world through the father's original guilt.

Since his metamorphosis, however, Gregor must assume the blame for this state of affairs. He alone now appears to be the cause of the whole "misfortune" of his family—unique as it is "in the entire circle of their relatives and acquaintances." He is guilty in a manner which lifts his "guilt" completely out of the sphere in which a socioeconomic interpretation could still be relevant. To be sure, in consequence of its economic impoverishment, the family disintegrates as a natural community. So far the analogy to Marx's world view holds. However, the limits of such an analogy are reached as soon as we realize that the ultimate cause of this proletarianization is a circumstance that transcends the observable laws of nature. In the midst of an environment which otherwise seems to be wholly determined by socioeconomic factors, Gregor's metamorphosis supplies the evidence of something inexplicable in, and therefore transcendent of, the terms of that *Weltbild.*

Mythic thinking also underlies Marx's view of history. Behind Marx's economic determinism one can glimpse the messianic martyr-savior's part played by the proletariat. In the world view of the young Marx especially, the proletariat suffers the fate and assumes the task of Christ. Today the proletariat is the scapegoat of humanity; tomorrow it will be its redeemer. So runs the Marxist myth. The proletariat will save the very society that has victimized it and committed the worst injustice against it. In his Preface to his "Critique of Hegel's *Philosophy of Law*," Marx states:

> In order that *one single estate* may stand for the condition of the whole society, all the defects of that society must be concentrated in one . . . class; a particular estate must be the estate of general offense, must be the embodiment of all frustrations; one particular social class must be seen as the *notorious crime* of the whole society, so that liberation of this class will appear to be the universal self-liberation.

In the microscopic society of his petty-bourgeois household, Gregor Samsa plays the same role that the proletariat, in Marx's vision, performs in the macroscopic social and universal society of the bourgeois-capitalist system.

The analogy between Gregor and the proletariat becomes clearer when we realize that Gregor's metamorphosis is bound up with "guilt" in a twofold way. The "guilt of the parents" is embodied *in* him; but it is also perpetrated *on* him. Insofar as his vermin appearance is the incarnation of parasitic selfishness, their guilt is embodied in him. However, insofar as he serves as the butt of the injustice and cruelty of his family, insofar as he suffers their total neglect and withdrawal of love, their guilt is perpetrated on him. As the unrecognized member of the family, Gregor corresponds to that universal victim of the capitalist order—the proletariat.

Gregor also exercises its eschatological function as the liberator and savior of his society. The "notorious crime" of society diagnosed by Marx as the surrender of man to inhumanity is embodied in the hero of Kafka's tale much more literally even than in the hero of Marx's view of history. Like the proletariat for Marx, Gregor bears in his family "radical chains." His existence, like the proletariat's, represents "the universal sorrows" of mankind. "No particular injustice," but "injustice as such" is committed against him. His very being, like that of the proletariat, proclaims "the total loss of humanity" —a loss that in his case manifests itself of course in its most literal meaning. Finally, like the proletariat in Marx's eschatological view of history, Gregor can regain his own humanity only by the liberation of his whole community.

However, in sharp contrast to Marx, the optimistic "synthesis" of self-liberation and liberation of all others is totally lacking in Kafka's world. Marx's proletariat redeems itself by redeeming mankind. In Kafka, liberation can be achieved only by the total sacrifice, the self-eradication of the scapegoat. Only by vanishing completely can Gregor save his family and himself.

While Marx's messianic view of the proletariat represents a secularized version of the Judaeo-Christian eschatology, the mythic dimension of Kafka's tale contradicts the latter. In the Christian version of the scapegoat myth, the savior's self-sacrifice is merely temporary. He arises again and takes the redeemed with him to eternal bliss. Kafka's myth follows the more primitive and universal "transference" myth which James George Frazer in *The Golden Bough* calls the myth of "the assassination of the god":

> The accumulated misfortunes and sins of the whole people are sometimes laid upon the dying god, who is supposed to bear them away forever, leaving the people innocent and happy. . . . It is not necessary that the evil should be transferred from the culprit or sufferer to a person; it may equally well be transferred to an animal or a thing.

In *The Metamorphosis*, "the guilt of the parents" has been transferred to Gregor. He is the scapegoat on whom the refuse, the filth, the "sin," of the whole community is deposited. This transference appears in him not only physically and externally as when the *Unrat* of the whole apartment is thrown into his room. It also shows itself inwardly as the—temporary—reprehensible and shocking deterioration of Gregor's character makes clear.

What remains for Gregor to do is to recognize that it is his role and mission "to bear away forever . . . the accumulated misfortunes and sins" of his family by removing himself in whom they are incarnated. In this lies the inner meaning of his metamorphosis which his sister's words make clear to him. "His opinion that he must disappear was if anything even more decided than his sister's."

He literally carries out the "turning," the spatial "return" "back into his room" that transposes *The Metamorphosis* from its economically determined foreground plot into the mythic frame from which it had issued. Hitherto intent on breaking out and returning to power, influence, love, and life, Gregor now withdraws forever into his room, into himself. He gives himself up to death by which he liberates not only the world from himself, but more importantly for Kafka, himself from the world.

The death of Gregor Samsa is self-imposed in the literal sense that it occurs only after the consent of the "hero." Gregor carries out the death sentence on himself that his sister, as the representative of the family and of life, has pronounced against him. He executes it by virtue of what can only be considered psychic power. He kills himself simply by his will— resembling in this respect Kleist's *Penthesilea*. His will is to obey the "law" which has chosen him for sacrifice so that his family can live free of *Schuld*, and the formulation of this will is immediately followed by its fulfillment— Gregor's death. It is a sacrificial death for the family of whom he thinks "with tenderness and love."

Kafka was satisfied with this death of his "hero," as his letter to Felice Bauer composed immediately after the writing of Gregor's death scene shows:

> Cry, Dearest, cry; now is the time for weeping! The hero of my little story died a short while ago. If it can console you, I shall tell you that he died quite peacefully and *reconciled* with all. (Italics and translation mine.)

The rhythm and the anaphoric structure of that first sentence resemble the lament for the "hero" of an epic of universal, at any rate of collective, significance. The "synthesis" expressed by the "consolation" of the third sentence is, in contrast to Marx's view of history, not the synthesis of fulfillment, but that of tragedy. Death as reconciliation implies not only the ancient idea of "atonement," but also the even more basic idea of the tragic as the sacrificial defeat of the individual in his ancient and eternal agon with the collective. This idea emerges as the "meaning" of the myth embedded in Kafka's story. The individual's extinction is balanced by his elevation and "eternalization" in the lament ("Now is the time for weeping") in which the intention of Kafka's "little story" appears to be summed up. Conversely, the sacrifice of the individual in whom "guilt" has become embodied, allows the community to enter upon a new life and entertain "new dreams." At the conclusion of the narrative text, Gregor's parents had grown

> more quiet and half unconsciously exchanging glances of agree-
> ment, that it would soon be time to find a good husband for
> [Grete]. And it was like a confirmation of their *new dreams* and
> *good intentions* that at the last stop of their trip their daughter got
> up first and stretched her young body. (Italics mine).

No matter how cruel and illusory the "new dreams" for the life of the daughter, purchased by the carcass of the son, may appear to be, about Kafka's unquali-fiedly affirmative evaluation of his "hero's" sacrificial death his letter to Felice leaves no doubt.

Kafka's definition of the writer's relationship to mankind applies to Gregor's role in the deliverance of his family.

> The writer is the scapegoat of humanity; he allows human beings
> to enjoy sin guiltlessly, almost guiltlessly.

In this sense, and in this sense alone, the mythos of *The Metamorphosis* describes a myth of literature. Gregor allows his family, as the writer allows humanity, to enjoy their guilt guiltlessly, which does *not* mean that he restores to them their innocence. They remain guilty, but they can now enjoy the fruits of this guilt without being held accountable. For the scapegoat who embodies their conscience makes them free of it.

Kafka and Sacher-Masoch

Mark M. Anderson

> "Das Attribut [des] grausamen Frauentypus ist dem Dichter das Vermächtnis Kains: Der Pelz."
>
> ["The attribute of the fearsome type of woman is, it seems to the writer, the inheritance of Cain: the furs."]
>
> (WANDA VON SACHER-MASOCH, in the foreword to *Die Dame im Pelz*)

> "Wir peitschen einander mit diesen häufigen Briefen."
>
> ["We are lashing each other with these frequent letters."]
>
> [KAFKA TO FELICE during the writing of *Die Verwandlung*, November 28, 1912)

On September 23, 1912, Kafka noted in his diary in regard to the writing of "Das Urteil":

> Viele während des Schreibens mitgefuhrte Gefuhle, zum Beispiel die Freude, dass ich etwas Schönes fur Maxens "Arkadia" haben werde, Gedanken an Freud natürlich, an einer Stelle an "Arnold Beer" an einer andern an Wassermann, an einer an Werfels "Riesin," natürlich auch an meine "Die städtische Welt."

> Many emotions carried along in the writing, joy, for example, that I shall have something beautiful for Max's *Arkadia*, thoughts about Freud, of course; in one passage, of *Arnold Beer*; in another, of Wasserman; in one, of Werfel's *Giantess*; of course, also of my "The Urban World."

> (*Franz Kafka: The Complete Stories*, edited by Nahum N. Glatzer and

From *The Kafka Society of America* 7, no. 2 (December 1983). © 1983 by the Kafka Society of America, Temple University.

translated by Willa Muir and Edwin Muir; all further references will
be to *The Complete Stories*)

He thus furnishes us with one of his few explicit comments on the literary
sources for his own writing, as well as an indication that this writing is highly
synthetic. A character, a peculiar gesture, a basic conflict between father and
son—these bits and pieces from other literary and nonliterary texts are sewn
together into a single text which appears to us uniquely "Kafkan," a seamless
artistic whole. And yet Kafka's text is not closed. Though it may well up
from and in some sense give expression to Kafka's personal life, "Das Urteil"
is nonetheless informed by a number of external sources.

The elation Kafka felt at having written his "breakthrough" story may
have been responsible for the revelation of its sources. With his other writings
Kafka was extremely chary in such information. Even to close friends such
as Max Brod or Felice Bauer he rarely spoke about the genesis of his literary
work. His diary is structured by a similar discretion and contains almost no
material that might be considered direct preparatory study for his finished
writings such as reading notes, outlines, sketches, or rough drafts. Yet there
is no reason to assume that Kafka's works are any less synthetic than "Das
Urteil," that for Kafka writing was not a gathering together of "mitgeführte
Gefühle" often related to past reading experiences. In fact, recent investigations have demonstrated that Kafka incorporated other literary texts, in a
strikingly direct manner, into his own writings although he makes no men-
tion of these texts or their authors in his diary and private correspondence.
In any case Kafka's secrecy in such matters (a secrecy which extends even
into his literary writings, inducing him to cover over the traces of his
predecessors) has helped foster a myth of unmitigated originality, as if Kafka's
texts were so unlike other works of literature, so peculiar to themselves, that
they could not have been significantly influenced by outside sources.

This conception of Kafka's originality has been reinforced by New Critical
or "textimmanent" interpretations which insist on the autonomy or closure
of the literary artifact. Few of the innumerable interpretations of Kafka's *Verwandlung*, for instance, address the question of the text's literary sources. In
fact, Stanley Corngold (who has helpfully assembled almost all published interpretations of Kafka's novella until 1970) characterizes the majority of these
readings as either symbolic or allegorical, and in his own interpretation largely
avoids the question of influence (*The Commentators' Despair*). Yet Kafka's critics
have been notoriously incapable of reaching agreement about his work. Unex-
plained, apparently unmotivated events, striking but impenetrable gestures,
dense verbal passages, etc. have stymied readers, thus providing them with

an excuse for one more interpretation. The question is whether the assumption that a literary text must be treated as an autonomous whole does not, in Kafka's case, predestine interpretive efforts to failure. For if the sources of these enigmatic elements lie outside the confines of Kafka's own writings, if he deliberately introduces "foreign" elements into his work without providing an aesthetic or cognitive framework through which their significance could be understood, then the critical effort to interpret this work only through itself can never achieve full explication.

The thesis of the present essay is that Kafka's texts are far less closed than they have traditionally been assumed to be and that Kafka's originality consists not so much in the invention of new literary forms as in the sewing together of preexisting materials, often of disparate origin. Cut out of their original context, deprived of the structure in which they were given meaning, these materials are incorporated into Kafka's own texts in more or less unmediated fashion. Thus they exist in their new surrounding as enigmatic ciphers, clearly imbued with significance but, because the traces of their origin have been obscured, they are difficult to interpret. The fabric of Kafka's writings presents itself as seamless, without origin; but if my hypothesis is correct, some of its densest visual and linguistic passages may stem from other hands. Their density is not inherent but a function of their discontinuous position in another signifying order. Emptied of the content they once possessed, they survive in Kafka's narrative as pure form, "allegorical" in Benjamin's sense of the term.

In support of this hypothesis I would point to the picture of the woman dressed in furs described at the opening of Kafka's *Verwandlung*:

> Über dem Tische . . . hing das Bild, das er von kurzem aus einer illustrierten Zeitschrift ausgeschnitten und in einem hübschen vergoldeten Rahmen untergebracht hatte. Es stellte eine Dame dar, die, mit einen Pelzhut und einer Pelzboa versehen, aufrecht dasass und einen schweren Pelzmuff, in dem ihr ganzer Unterarm verschwunden war, dem Beschauer entgegenhob.

> [Above the table . . . hung the picture which he had recently cut out of an illustrated magazine and put into a pretty gilt frame. It showed a lady with a fur cap on and a fur stole, sitting upright and holding out to the spectator a huge fur muff into which the whole of her forearm had vanished.]

This image is obviously central to the novella as a whole: the alacrity with which it is introduced into the narrative, the importance Gregor attaches to it in his struggles with his family, etc. suggest that if we could understand the significance of this representation we would be closer to an understanding of Gregor's metamorphosis. For the woman, like Gregor, seems to have disappeared, or is about to disappear, into an animal covering; her appearance in the second paragraph doubles Gregor's transformation in the first; and so her picture seems to function as the specular image of Gregor's own condition.

But it is difficult, on the basis of the *Verwandlung*'s plot, to assess the significance of this resemblance. That Gregor and the woman are somehow allied against the family becomes clear at the end of the second section when he tries to save her picture during the "invasion" of his room by mother and sister. But after this episode the picture disappears. Gregor's desire shifts in the third section to his violin-playing sister, and it is not even clear whether the picture is still in Gregor's room. Thus the novella ends with that thread (and not only that thread) untied, an unsolved puzzle. Of obvious significance to Gregor and, implicitly, to the narrator, the picture of the fur-clad woman remains incomprehensible to his family and, of course, the reader.

What I will attempt to demonstrate in the following remarks is that Kafka transposed this picture from a popular novel of his period, namely, Sacher-Masoch's *Venus im Pelz*. This work, which was originally published as part of the collection *Das Vermächtnis Kains* (*The Legacy of Cain*) in 1870, then reprinted separately and translated into many languages, owed much of its success to its depiction of a sado-masochistic relationship between two Hapsburg aristocrats, Severin von Kusiemski and Wanda von Dunajew. I will also show that Sacher-Masoch's novel influenced Kafka's writing of the *Verwandlung* in many respects besides this picture, indeed, more than any of the commonly accepted sources such as Gogol's "The Nose" or Dostoevsky's *The Double* (compare Spilka and Binder). To demonstrate this influence I will first elaborate the numerous points of contact between these two works, noting where Kafka followed Sacher-Masoch but also where he deviated from him. Secondly, I will pose the more general question of how an understanding of this influence allows for a rethinking of the meaning of Kafka's novella as a whole.

As its title indicates, the protagonist of Sacher-Masoch's novel is a beautiful woman dressed in furs. One of the many descriptions of "Venus" that may have caught Kafka's attention is the following, which appears near the novel's beginning in a dialogue between Severin and an unnamed narrator:

> Ein schönes Weib . . . ruhte, auf den linken Arm gestützt, nackt
> in einem dunklen Pelz auf einer Ottomane; ihre rechte Hand

spielte mit einer Peitsche, während ihr blosser Fuss sich nachlässig auf den Mann stützte, der vor ihr lag wie ein Sklave, wie ein Hund, und dieser Mann, mit den scharfen, aber wohlgebildeteten Zügen, auf denen brütende Schwermut und hingebende Leidenschaft lag, welcher mit dem schwärmerischen brennenden Auge eines Märtyrers zu ihr emporsah, dieser Mann, der den Schemel ihrer Füsse bildete, war Severin. . . .

"Venus im Pelz!" rief ich, auf das Bild deutend, "so habe ich sie im Traume gesehen."

"Ich auch," sagte Severin, "nur habe ich meinen Traum mit offenen Augen geträumt."

[A beautiful woman . . . was resting on an ottoman, supported on her left arm. She was nude in her dark furs. Her right hand played with a lash, while her bare foot rested carelessly on a man, lying before her like a slave, like a dog. In the sharply outlined but well-formed lineaments of this man lay a brooding melancholy and passionate devotion; he looked up to her with the ecstatic burning eye of a martyr. This man, the footstool for her feet, was Severin. . . .

Venus in Furs," I cried, pointing to the picture. "That is the way I saw her in my dream."

"I too," said Severin, "only I dreamed my dream with open eyes."]

(Leopold Von Sacher-Masoch, *Venus in Furs,* translated by Fernanda Savage)

Gregor's transformation into vermin form is not directly paralleled in Sacher-Masoch's novel. But the crux of this work (as well as the source of its notoriety) was the depiction of a masochistic love relationship which metamorphosed its participants into "animals." Venus's fur clothes serve as the visual catalyst as well as the symbol for this transformation. Draped in animal skins, she is repeatedly characterized as a cat, a she-wolf, a she-bear, a tigress, etc. Severin, the willing victim in the relationship, descends from his aristocratic position of equality with Wanda (Venus's actual name) to become her "slave," her "donkey," her "dog," her "worm"; any less than human form which must submit to her will and can be physically abused — whipped, kicked, trodden underfoot, etc.

The first time Severin is whipped by Wanda, that is, the first time they fully assume their "animal" roles, Severin is later troubled by "troubled dreams":

Nachdem ich die Nacht wie im Fieber in wirren Träumen gelegen, bin ich erwacht. Es dämmert kaum.

Was ist wahr von dem, was in meiner Erinnerung schwebt? Was habe ich erlebt und was nur geträumt? Gepeitscht bin ich worden, das ist gewiss, ich fühle noch jeden einzelnen Hieb, ich kann die roten, brennenden Streifen an meinem Leib zählen. Und *sie* hat mich gepeitscht. Ja, jetzt weiss ich alles.

Meine Phantasie ist Wahrheit geworden.

[After having spent a feverish night filled with confused dreams, I awoke. Dawn was just beginning to break.

How much of what was hovering in my memory was true? What had I actually experienced and what had I dreamed? That I had been whipped was certain. I can still feel each blow, and count the burning red stripes on my body. And *she* whipped me. Now I know everything.

My dream had become truth.]

This passage directly recalls the celebrated opening of Kafka's novella: "Als Gregor Samsa eines Morgens aus unruhigen Träumen erwachte, fand er sich in seinem Bett zu einem ungeheuren Ungeziefer verwandelt" ["As Gregor Samsa awoke one morning from uneasy dreams he found himself transformed in his bed into a giant insect"]. Both protagonists awake from "troubled dreams" to find the corporeal evidence of their new identity, Gregor in his reptile shell, Severin in the whip marks demonstrating his animal subjugation to his mistress. Further, the arched segments on Gregor's belly bear a certain resemblance to the "burning red stripes" on Severin's body. As in Kafka's text, we find here the play between image and dream, and in both cases the reality of the former over the latter is affirmed. "Es war kein Traum" ["It was no dream"] we are informed at the outset of Gregor's metamorphosis; "Meine Phantasie ist Wahrheit geworden," [see above] Severin reflects.

Sacher-Masoch's novel prepares the reader for Severin's transformation, thus explaining it and to a certain extent diminishing its effect on the reader. Kafka's novella begins abruptly with Gregor's metamorphosis, shocking the reader with an apparently unmotivated but incontrovertible absurdity. It pointedly omits an explanation for this transformation, and this omission is obviously a key element of the narrative strategy. However, later in the story we learn from Gregor's mother that, like Severin, Gregor has been "involved" with the lady in furs. She relates to the chief clerk that Gregor's only evening "distraction" ("Zerstreuung") from the reading of newspapers and train timetables has been his "fretwork" ("Laubsägearbeit"), carried out in the solitude of his room. She adds that in the course of several evenings previous to his metamorphosis Gregor carved a handsome, gilded frame for his picture which now hangs in his room. This reference, seen against the backdrop of Sacher-Masoch's novel, suggests a connection between Gregor's metamorphosis and his evening "Zerstreuung" with the woman in furs, a point which will be developed in the conclusion to the present essay.

The parallel with Sacher-Masoch's *Venus im Pelz* allows us to reconsider the spatial dynamics of Kafka's opening paragraphs. The photograph of the woman in furs is positioned on the wall above the table, presumably opposite Gregor's bed. The woman is sitting upright and seems to be threatening Gregor (who at that moment is the only "spectator" in the room), with her heavy fur muff: "[das Bild] stellte eine Dame dar, die . . . einen schweren Pelzmuff . . . dem Beschauer entgegenhob" ["It showed a lady . . . holding out to the spectator a huge fur muff"]. Gregor, for his part, is helplessly imprisoned in his bed by his vermin form. His legs flutter "helplessly," he wants to "free himself from his bed," but all his efforts initially fail. Moreover, Gregor's struggles result in the experiencing of a pain never felt before:

> Mit welcher Kraft er sich auf die rechte Seite warf, immer wieder schaukelte er in die Rückenlage zurück. Er versuchte es wohl hundertmal . . . und liess erst ab, als er . . . einen noch nie gefühlten, leichten, dumpfen Schmerz zu fühlen begann.

> [However violently he forced himself toward his right side, he always rolled onto his back again. He tried at least a hundred times . . . and only desisted when he began to feel . . . a faint dull ache he had never experienced before.]

Thus, if one is willing to grant the woman in the photograph a certain reality, one may say that the *Verwandlung* begins with a scene of domination much like those repeatedly described in Sacher-Masoch's *Venus im Pelz*: a man-animal lies "tied," in pain, to his bed while a woman dressed in furs raises a threatening fist above him.

In Kafka's *Verwandlung* it is not immediately clear what erotic tie exists between Gregor and the fur-clad woman in the picture. But this tie is made explicit as the story develops. We learn from Gregor's mother that rather than go out he has spent several evenings alone in his room with his picture. Later, when Gregor's mother and sister are cleaning out his room, he reflects on what is most dear to him and decides to save "at least" the picture:

Er wusste wirklich nicht, was er zuerst retten sollte, da sah er an der im übrigen schon leeren Wand auffallend das Bild der in lauter Pelzwerk gekleideten Dame hängen, kroch eilends hinauf und presste sich an das Glas, das ihn festhielt und seinem heissen Bauch wohltat. Dieses Bild wenigstens, das Gregor jetzt ganz verdeckte, würde nun gewiss niemand wegnehmen.

[Then on the wall opposite, which was already otherwise cleared, he was struck by the picture of the lady muffed in so much fur, and quickly crawled up to it and pressed himself to the glass, which was a good surface to hold on to and comforted his hot belly. The picture at least, which was entirely hidden beneath him, was not going to be removed by anybody.]

The erotic nature of this moment—the glass which holds Gregor "tight" like a lover's embrace, the cooling of his "hot stomach" on the glass, etc.—is unmistakable. The striking fact of this union, of course, is that it takes place between Gregor and a picture rather than with another person (or character). In Sacher-Masoch's novel, Severin admits that his first erotic ideal was not an actual woman but a representation: "Ein Jude, der mit Photographien handelt, spielt mir das Bild meines Ideals in die Hände. . . . Welch ein Weib! Ich will ein Gedicht machen. Nein! Ich nehme das Blatt und schreibe dazu: "*Venus im Pelz*" ["Through a Jew, dealing in photographs, I secured a picture of my ideal . . . . What a woman! I want to write a poem but instead I take the reproduction and write on it: *Venus in Furs*"]. From this moment on Severin develops a passion for all representation of cruelty and domination:

Ich las fortan mit einer wahren Gier Geschichten, in denen die furchtbarsten Grausamkeiten geschildert, und sah mit besonderer Lust Bilder, Stiche, auf denen sie zur Darstellung kamen."

[I developed a perfect passion for reading stories in which the extremest cruelties were described. I loved especially to look at pictures and prints which represented them.]

Perhaps the strongest piece of evidence demonstrating Kafka's knowledge and use of Sacher-Masoch's work may be found in the similarity of names. When Severin agrees to become Wanda's slave, wearing a uniform with her colors and coat of arms, she decides to rebaptize him. Henceforth he is to be addressed only with the familiar "Du" and a new first name:

"Ich verbitte mir jede Vertraulichkeit," sagte sie. . . .

"Sie heissen von nun an hicht mehr Severin, sondern *Gregor*."
Ich bebte vor Wut und doch—ich kann es leider nicht leugenen—auch vor Genuss und prickelnder Aufregung."

["I forbid any sort of familiarity," she said. . . . "From now on your name is no longer Severin, but *Gregor*."
"I trembled with rage, and yet, unfortunately, I cannot deny it, I also felt a strange pleasure and stimulation."]

Sacher-Masoch himself signed a similar contract with his wife, also changing his name to Gregor which, according to his biographer, "was a typical name for a manservant in this part of Austria" (James Cleugh, *The First Masochist*). Further, Severin's fate is repeatedly compared to that of Samson: once when he meets his mistress, once again when he signs a legal contract establishing his status as her slave, and finally at the novel's conclusion when, like the Old Testament hero, he is betrayed by the woman he loves. Thus Severin in the hands of his mistress becomes Gregor/Samson. The similarity between the two names is striking, if admittedly less so in German where Samson is called "Simson." Kafka himself explicitly compares himself to Samson in a letter to Milena ("So jetzt hat Simson Dalila sein Geheimnis erzählt und sie kann ihm die Haare . . . auch abschneiden" ["Now Samson has told Delilah his secret, and she can cut off his hair as well"]). And in any case, Kafka would have modified the name to correspond to his own, much as he had with Georg *Bende*-mann in "Das Urteil" (see *Tagebücher*). Summing up, one might say that Kafka typically adapts Sacher-Masoch's novel for his own purposes by condensing it; he begins his novella with the abrupt fact of Gregor's "enslavement." Later Gregor will be denied even the name of a servant.

By this point another of Kafka's innovations will have become clear: namely, that what in Sacher-Masoch's novel is fundamentally a dialectic of submission between a male slave and a female mistress operates, in Kafka's novella, on two levels. The opening scene depicts Gregor, like Gregor-Severin at the feet of Wanda, as dominated by the woman in furs. But as the story develops this domination is increasingly exercised by Gregor's family. However, the erotic and masochistic elements of this relationship remain intact. Thus Kafka seems to have taken the basic situation described in *Venus im Pelz* for the opening of his text (almost as a visual cue), reinserting it into the context of Gregor's oedipal relationship with his family. This fusion of Sacher-Masoch with Freud will be dealt with more thoroughly below.

In Sacher-Masoch's novel Gregor-Severin is bound by a legal contract which makes him his mistress's chattel. This is first of all a financial dependence:

"Aber, Sie kennen doch meine Verhältnisse, gnädige Frau,"
begann ich verwirrt, "ich bin noch von meinem Vater abhängig
und zweifle, dass er mir eine so grosse Summe als ich zu dieser
Reise brauche—."

"Das heisst, du hast kein Geld, Gregor," bemerkte Wanda
vergnügt, "um so besser, dann bist du vollkommen von mir
abhängig und in der Tat mein Sklave."

["But, madame, you know my circumstances," I began in my
confusion. "I am dependent on my father, and I doubt whether
he will give me the large sum of money needed for this journey—."
"That means you have no money, Gregor," said Wanda
delightedly. "So much the better, you are then entirely dependent
on me, and in fact my slave."]

In Kafka's story, Gregor is kept from quitting his work as a commercial
salesman by his father's debts ("Schulden"), which must be paid off to preserve
the family's good name. After his metamorphosis Gregor becomes entirely
dependent on his family and must accept the garbage given to him as food,
which he is no longer capable of earning. An important discrepancy, however,
should not go unnoticed. Whereas Gregor-Severin becomes a slave, thereby
firmly establishing his identity through that of his mistress, Gregor Samsa's
transformation into an unnameable vermin releases him from family and office
obligations—from that world of "traffic" he denigrates at the outset of the
story as a "nie herzlich werdender menschlicher Verkehr" ["business which
never grows genuinely human"]. Gregor Samsa as beetle has no work function
in society, is thus without identity, and cannot be considered a slave. However,
Gregor's father, who takes on a job as a liveried bank messenger after his
son's transformation, sleeps in his uniform and defines his identity through
the authority of his employer, closely resembles Gregor-Severin in Sacher-
Masoch's work (who dons the uniform of his mistress). One of the paradoxes
of Kafka's *Verwandlung*, and one of the ways it reverses its source, is that
Gregor's metamorphosis brings about the enslavement of those who once
enslaved him.

The most salient aspect of *Venus im Pelz*, however, which prompted
Krafft-Ebing to grant Sacher-Masoch unwanted fame in the annals of
psychological medicine, is the link in masochistic behavior between domination
and sexual pleasure. Gregor-Severin experiences sexual pleasure when he is
physically humiliated and dominated by his mistress. This punishment
invariably follows the same scenario: Wanda dresses in furs, binds her lover,

and whips him until he cries for mercy. The fur clothing is essential to this process and is also related to Kafka's *Verwandlung* in one striking detail; Gregor-Severin describes its symbolic importance in the following learned dialogue:

> "Pelzwerk [übt] auf alle nervösen Naturen eine aufregende Wirkung, welche auf ebenso allgemeinen als natürlichen Gesetzen beruht. . . . Die Wissenschaft hat in neuester Zeit eine gewisse Verwandtschaft zwischen Elektrizität und Wärme nachgewiesen. . . . Daher der hexenhaft wohltätige Einfluss, welchen die Gesellschaft von Katzen auf reizbare geistige Menschen übt und diese langgeschwänzten Grazien der Tierwelt, diese niedlichen, funkensprühenden, elektrischen Batterien zu den Lieblingen eines Mahomed, Kardinal Richelieu, Crebillon, Rousseau, Wieland gemacht hat."
>
> "Eine Frau, die also einen Pelz trägt," rief Wanda, "ist also nichts anderes als eine grosse Katze, eine verstärkte elektrische Batterie?"
>
> "Gewiss," erwiderte ich.

> ["Furthermore, furs have a stimulating effect on all highly organized natures. This is due to both general and natural laws. . . . Science has recently shown a certain relationship between electricity and warmth. . . . This is the reason why the presence of cats exercises such a magic influence upon highly organized men of intellect. This is why these long-tailed Graces of the animal kingdom, these adorable, scintillating electric batteries have been the favorite animal of a Mohammed, Cardinal Richelieu, Crebillon, Rousseau, Wieland."
>
> "A woman wearing furs, then," cried Wanda, "is nothing else than a large cat, an augmented electric battery?"
>
> "Certainly," I replied.]

The connection between furs and electricity is surprising. More than just the symbol of power, wealth, beauty; more than just the tactile agent in the erotic metamorphosis into animal forms, furs also bring to Gregor-Severin's mind the unpredictable, dangerous energy of electricity. Like a cat's claws emerging suddenly from its paws, or the stinging lash of a whip experienced by a blindfolded victim, furs appeal to the masochist for the mystery of what they might conceal: unexpected, intense, and therefore pleasurable pain.

Perhaps the cruelest whipping scene in Sacher-Masoch's novel takes place in the conclusion. Not only is Gregor-Severin bound and whipped by his lover; but suddenly his *rival*, a handsome and rich Greek dubbed Apollo, emerges from the closed canopy of her bed in order to whip him himself. This final betrayal and humiliation initially provoke Gregor-Severin's terror, then his sense of humor:

> Ich war anfangs sprachlos, starr. Die Situation war entsetzlich komisch, ich hätte selbst laut aufgelacht, wenn sie nicht zugleich so verzweifelt traurig, so schmachvoll für mich gewesen wäre.

> [At first I was speechless, petrified. There was a horribly comic element in the situation. I would have laughed out loud had not my position been at the same time so terribly cruel and humiliating.]

As the Greek prepares to flay Gregor-Severin, the latter glances at a picture hanging in the bedroom where "Simson zu Delilas Füssen von den Philistern geblendet wird. Das Bild erschien mir in diesem Augenblick wie ein Symbol, ein ewiges Gleichnis der Leidenschaft, der Wollust, der Liebe des Mannes zum Weibe" ["Lying at Delilah's feet, Samson was about to have his eyes put out by the Philistines. The picture at the moment seemed to me like a symbol, an eternal parable of passion and lust, of the love of man for woman"]. Then the Greek begins to whip Gregor-Severin while Wanda lies half-naked in her furs on on the ottoman, convulsed with laughter. Gregor-Severin almost "verging vor Scham und Verzweiflung" ["died with shame and despair"]; but he also admits to feeling "eine Art phantastischen, übersinnlichen Reiz" ["a certain wild supersensual stimulation"] under Apollo's whip and the cruel laughter of his Venus. Curled up "wie ein Wurm, den man zertritt" ["like a worm that is trodden on"], his wounds flowing, he suddenly realizes

> mit entsetzlicher Klarheit, wohin die blinde Leidenschaft, die Wollust, seit Holofernes und Agamemnon den Mann geführt hat, in den Sack, in das Netz des verräterischen Weibes, in Elend, Sklaverei und Tod.
> Mir was es, wie das Erwachen aus einem Traum.

> [with horrible clarity, whither blind passion and lust have led man, ever since Holofernes and Agamemnon—driven into a sack, into the net of woman's treachery, into misery, slavery and death.
> It was like waking from a dream.]

Wanda and Apollo abandon him, and the novel draws to a rapid end.
One might initially object that Kafka's text offers no equivalent scene

of bondage and flagellation at the hand of one's sexual rival. But almost every key element in Sacher-Masoch's concluding scenario is reproduced in the final scene of the second chapter of *Verwandlung*. Blindness, "electric" flagellation, sexual union of lover and rival—all of these aspects come into play when Gregor's father begins pelting him with apples. This punishment, it should be recalled, has been precipitated by Gregor's obscene coupling with the picture of his "Venus in Furs," which causes his mother to faint and his father to lose all patience. As in *Venus im Pelz*, Gregor's predicament is at once terrible and comic:

> Da flog knapp neben ihm, leicht geschleudert, irgend etwas nieder und rollte vor ihm her. Es war ein Apfel; gleich flog ihm ein zweiter nach; Gregor blieb vor Schrecken stehen; ein Weiterlaufen war nutzlos, denn der Vater hatte sich entschlossen, ihn zu bombardieren.

> [Suddenly something lightly flung landed close behind him and rolled before him. It was an apple; a second apple followed immediately; Gregor came to a stop in alarm; there was no point in running on for his father was determined to bombard him.]

Strangely enough, these apples have an electric charge; they roll "wie elektrisiert auf dem Boden herum und stiessen aneinander" ["about the floor as if magnetized and cannoned into each other]. The biblical significance of the apples is evident and has been amply discussed. But their unusual electric charge, which cannot be explained by Kafka's text alone and has been skipped over by most commentators, establishes another link with the electric furs in Sacher-Masoch's whipping scenarios. In Kafka's text the apples rain down like lashes of a whip on Gregor's back, piercing his shell, and inducing an "überraschende[n] unglaubliche[n] Schmerz" ["startling, incredible pain"]. One of them bores into his back ("*drang* . . . förmlich in Gregors Rücken *ein*" ["literally penetrated Gregor's back"], my emphasis), where it later becomes encrusted. And although Gregor "wants" to move away in order to decrease the pain, instead he stretches himself out, "wie festgenagelt" ["as if nailed down"], to receive his father's blows. More than just a reference to Christ's crucifixion, the word "festgenagelt" reiterates the painful penetration of Gregor's body by a sharp object as well as, on an unconscious level, Gregor's willingness to submit to corporal punishment. The beating delivered by the father comes as a secretly desired judgment.

At this point Gregor begins to go blind. With his last look he sees how his mother, whose dress has already been taken off by Grete, rushes to her husband, tripping over the petticoats which she loses on the way, to unite with him in a clearly sexual union:

> Nur mit dem letzten Blick sah er noch . . . wie dann die Mutter auf den Vater zulief und ihr auf dem Weg die aufgebundenen Röcke einer nach dem anderen zu Boden glitten, und wie sie stolpernd über die Röcke auf den Vater eindrang und ihn umarmend, in gänzlicher Vereinigung mit ihm — nun versagte Gregors Sehkraft schon — die Hände an des Vaters Hinterkopf um Schonung von Gregors Leben bat.

> [With his last conscious look . . . he saw his mother rushing toward his father, leaving one after another behind her on the floor her loosened petticoats, stumbling over her petticoats straight to his father and embracing him, in complete union with him — but here Gregor's sight began to fail — with her hands clasped around his father's neck as she begged for her son's life.]

Like the Samson in Sacher-Masoch's novel, whose destiny seems to Gregor-Severin a parable of passion and lust, Kafka's Gregor loses his vision at the hand of the "Philistines," his uncomprehending family members (compare Holland). In *Venus im Pelz* the rival is Apollo, the strong and handsome Greek; in Kafka's *Verwandlung* Gregor's father is a clearly sexual rival to his son. Both protagonists must look on helplessly while their rivals enjoy the sexual favors of their unattainable objects of desire: Wanda in Sacher-Masoch's novel and, in Kafka's version, Gregor's mother. And in both cases the trauma of this *Urszene* results in blindness.

The major discrepancy between the two versions is that in *Venus im Pelz* Wanda abandons Gregor-Severin with his rival, whereas in *Die Verwandlung* Gregor's mother pleads with her husband to spare their son's life. But the triangle of desire and punishment is the same in both texts: on the one hand the familial (or oedipal) triangles of father, mother, and son; on the other Sacher-Masoch's triangle of masochistic victim, punishing rival and female lover. But for Kafka, who knew Freud's theories on the sexual rivalry between the father and son, these triangles were not essentially different. Indeed, on the basis of the present comparison we may say that the distinctive power of his *Verwandlung* would seem to result from its fusion of the writings of both Freud and Sacher-Masoch. Masochism is the decisive element of difference in Kafka's "Freudian" depiction of Gregor's familial ties, the element that transforms Gregor's "failure" to resolve his oedipal complex into a source of pleasure.

Venus im Pelz and *Die Verwandlung* diverge strikingly in their conclusions. Gregor-Severin is "cured" by his beating, returns home to inherit his father's belongings, and learns to assume the dominant role of a tyrant. He moralizes that "das Weib, wie es die Natur geschaffen und wie es der Mann gegenwärtig heranzieht, sein Feind ist und nur seine Sklavin oder seine Despot in sein kann, nie aber seine Gafährtin" ["woman, as nature has created her and as man is at present educating her, is his enemy. She can only be his slave or his despot, but never his companion"]. And, in a final allusion to Goethe, Severin concludes:

> "Jetzt haben wir nur die Wahl, Hammer oder Amboss zu sein, und ich war der Esel, aus mir den Sklaven eines Weibes zu machen, verstehst du?
> Daher die Moral der Geschichte: wer sich peitschen lässt, verdient, gepeitscht zu werden."

> ["At present, we have only the choice of being hammer or anvil, and I was the kind of donkey who let a woman make a slave of him, do you understand?
> The moral of the tale is this: whoever allows himself to be whipped, deserves to be whipped."]

Kafka's Gregor, of course, never learns to assume a dominant role in his family struggle. Rather, his punishment and humiliation increase until he is finally denied even the marginal humanity implicit in his first name; he becomes a thing, an undifferentiated, neuter "es" completely excluded from family and social ties. This final rejection is meted out by Grete, Gregor's beloved sister:

> "Weg muss er," rief die Schwester, "das ist das einzige Mittel, Vater. Du musst bloss den Gedanken loszuwerden suchen, dass es Gregor ist.

> ["He must go," cried Gregor's sister, "that's the only solution, Father. You must just try to get rid of the idea that this is Gregor."]

Shortly thereafter, Gregor makes the discovery that he is incapable of any physical movement. He has grown "comfortable" ("behaglich") with the pain in his body. He resolves to disappear, apparently having accepted the moral of Sacher-Masoch's tale that "whoever allows himself to be whipped, deserves to be whipped." He thinks once more of his family with tenderness and love. "In diesem Zustande leeren und friedlichen Nachdenkens blieb er, bis die

Turmuhr die dritte Morgenstunde schlug" ["In this state of vacant and peaceful meditation he remained until the clock tower struck three in the morning"]. The striking of the clock signals his death. It is in, a sense, Gregor's final beating.

Kafka's *Verwandlung* has not generally been read through the eyes of a masochist. Rather, Gregor's metamorphosis into an unnameable vermin form has most often been interpreted as a calamity, as punishment meted out for no obvious crime. But if we read the story through the eyes of Sacher-Masoch, then it is possible to see how this punishment, as brutal or warranted as it may initially appear, contains an element of pleasure, indeed, of erotic pleasure. Why, we must ask, does Kafka write clearly autobiographical works in which he is repeatedly humiliated, punished, exposed, mistreated? And why do his heroes repeatedly accept, even welcome, such treatment? The component of masochistic pleasure in Kafka's writings has not been completely ignored, but, on the basis of Kafka's direct relation to Sacher-Masoch, needs to be reformulated with greater precision and force. As a final point of commentary on this problem we may quote Kafka's letter to Felice of November 23–24, 1912, in which he calls his *Verwandlung* an "ekelhafte Geschichte" but describes the *writing* of it as an extremely "wollüstiges Geschäft."

On a biographical level, the picture of the woman in furs clearly corresponds to Felice Bauer who, because she lived in Berlin, was present to Kafka only in the form of a representation: in her letters and most of all in Kafka's mental picture of her during their brief encounters. Moreover, photographic representations were crucial erotic factors in their relationship. Their first contact was at Max Brod's home while looking at photographs of Palestine (*Briefe an Felice*). (*Die Verwandlung* was begun on November 17.) Four days later he mentions the photograph she has sent him, adding that it accompanies him on his business travels into hotel rooms. On December 10 (three days after finishing the *Verwandlung*), Kafka writes of kissing Felice's picture: "Einen langen Kuss auf den wehmütigen Mund des Mädchens auf der letzten Photographie" ["A long kiss on the melancholy mouth of the girl in the most recent photograph"]. What this parallel between text and life suggests is the utopic function of the photograph as a window, a promise, an "Ausweg" from the familial, oedipal situation. Just as Gregor Samsa yearns to escape from office responsibilities and familial "Schulden," so is Kafka's entire relationship to Felice colored by the notion of a utopic escape from Prague to Berlin or Palestine. And in both instances the promise represented by these photographs aids the cause of filial "revolt."

That this revolt should result in another form of passive enslavement is only one of the many paradoxes in Kafka's writings. The above remarks are meant only as preliminary speculations on the general impact of Sacher-Masoch's novel on the *Verwandlung*. Obviously, their relevance depends on whether one accepts Sacher-Masoch's novel as a source for Kafka's masterpiece. In view of this condition, I would like to conclude with one final piece of "circumstantial" evidence. As mentioned earlier, Kafka makes no direct reference to Sacher-Masoch in his writings. But in August 1913, nine months after the writing of *Verwandlung* and at the height of his personal troubles with Felice, Kafka wrote the beginning of a dramatic dialogue between a middle-aged married couple in his diary. The dialogue breaks off too soon for us to interpret its content other than that it clearly relates to Kafka's misapprehensions about the prospect of marriage with Felice. But the characters' names (always a key element in Kafka's writings) give us a hint of what the play might have been about. The woman is named Felice S., and clearly refers to Felice Bauer. Her husband is named Leopold S. So far as I know, this name never recurs in Kafka's other writings. What I hope the present essay has demonstrated is that this name must refer not only to Kafka but also to Leopold von S[acher-Masoch], and that Kafka was here (as in his *Verwandlung*), once more consciously identifying with the author of *Venus im Pelz*. Sacher-Masoch's novel is not only a source for *Die Verwandlung*; it is also the magnifying glass through which Kafka interpreted and structured the text of his own life.

Chronology

1883	Born in Prague on July 3.
1889–93	Attends German elementary school.
1893–1901	Attends German Staatsgymnasium.
1901–6	Studies law at the German Karl-Ferdinand University in Prague.
1902	Meets Max Brod.
1904	Begins *Description of a Struggle*.
1906	Starts working in a law office as a secretary. Receives law degree. Embarks on his year of practical training in Prague law courts.
1907	Writes "Wedding Preparations in the Country." Takes temporary position with Assurazioni Generali.
1908	Eight prose pieces published under the title *Betrachtung (Meditation)*. Accepts position with Workers' Accident Insurance Institute.
1909	Two sketches (originally part of *Description of a Struggle*) published. Trip to Riva and Brescia (with Max and Otto Brod). "Die Aeroplane in Brescia" published.
1910	Five prose pieces published under the title *Betrachtung (Meditation)* Starts diary. Trip to Paris (with Max and Otto Brod). Visit to Berlin.
1911	Official trip to Bohemia. Trip (with Max Brod) to Switzerland, Italy, and France, writing travelogues. Becomes interested in Yiddish theatre and literature.
1912	Starts working on *Amerika*. Visits Leipzig and Weimar (with Max Brod). Meets Felice Bauer. Writes "The Judgment." Writes *The Metamorphosis*. *Meditation* published.
1913	"The Stoker" published. Visits Felice Bauer in Berlin. "The Judgment" published. Travels to Vienna and Italy.

1914   Engagement to Felice Bauer. Breaks off engagement. Visit to Germany. Starts *The Trial.* Writes "In the Penal Colony."

1915   Reconciliation with Felice Bauer. *The Metamorphosis* published.

1916   Resumes writing after two years' silence: the fragments of "The Hunter Gracchus," "A Country Doctor," and other stories later included in *A Country Doctor.*

1917   Writing stories, among others "A Report to an Academy," "The Cares of a Family Man," and "The Great Wall of China." Re-engagement to Felice Bauer. Tuberculosis diagnosed. Takes extended sick leave. Engagement to Felice Bauer broken off again.

1918   Continued ill health. Intermittent stays at sanatoria.

1919   Brief engagement to Julie Wohryzek. "In the Penal Colony" and *A Country Doctor* published. Writes "Letter to His Father."

1920   Begins correspondence with Milena Jesenská. Intermittent stays at sanatoria.

1921   Goes back to work with the Workers' Accident Insurance Institute. "The Bucket Rider" published.

1922   Writes *The Castle,* "A Hunger Artist," "Investigations of a Dog." Breaks off relations with Milena Jesenská. Retires from Workers' Accident Insurance Institute. "A Hunger Artist" published.

1923   Meets Dora Dymant. Goes to live with Dora Dymant in Berlin. Writes "The Burrow."

1924   Moves back to Prague and writes "Josephine the Singer." Moves to Sanatorium Wiener Wald near Vienna. Dies at Sanatorium Kierling also near Vienna. Buried in Prague. Collection *A Hunger Artist* published shortly after his death.

Contributors

HAROLD BLOOM, Sterling Professor of the Humanities at Yale University, is the author of *The Anxiety of Influence*, *Poetry and Repression*, and many other volumes of literary criticism. His forthcoming study, *Freud: Transference and Authority*, attempts a full-scale reading of all of Freud's major writings. A MacArthur Prize Fellow, he is general editor of five series of literary criticism published by Chelsea House. During 1987–88, he served as Charles Eliot Norton Professor of Poetry at Harvard University.

MARTIN GREENBERG is Professor of English at Long Island University. He has written extensively on science-fiction and is the author of *Coming Attractions* as well as several science-fiction anthologies.

STANLEY CORNGOLD is Professor of German and Comparative Literature at Princeton University. A leading Kafka scholar, he is the author of *The Commentators' Despair: The Interpretation of Kafka's* Metamorphosis and the editor of an annotated critical edition of *The Metamorphosis*.

EVELYN TORTON BECK teaches Comparative Literature, German and Women's Studies at the University of Wisconsin, Madison. Her books include *Kafka and the Yiddish Theatre: Its Impact on His Work*, *Interpretive Synthesis*, *Nice Jewish Girls: A Lesbian Anthology*, and *The Prism of Sex*.

RONALD GRAY is J. R. R. Tolkien Professor of English at Oxford. Among his many critical studies in German Literature are *Goethe the Alchemist*, *The German Tradition in Literature*, and *Brecht the Dramatist*.

DAVID EGGENSCHWILER teaches English at the University of Southern California and is the author of *The Christian Humanism of Flannery O'Connor*.

ROY PASCAL was Professor of German at Cambridge University before his death in 1980. His books include *From Naturalism to Expressionism: German Literature and Society*, *The Dual Voice*, *The Nazi Dictatorship*, and *Design and Truth in Autobiography*.

WALTER H. SOKEL is Commonwealth Professor of German Language and English Literature at the University of Virginia. In addition to his many books and articles on Franz Kafka, he has published *The Writer in Extremis: Expressionism in Twentieth Century German Literature.*

MARK M. ANDERSON teaches in the German department at Columbia University. He is the author of *The Broken Boat* and *In the Storm of Roses: Selected Poems by Ingeborg Bachmann.*

Bibliography

Adams, Robert M. *Strains of Discord*, 168–79. Ithaca: Cornell University Press, 1958.

Adorno, Theodor W. "Notes on Kafka." In *Prisms*. Translated by Samuel Weber and Shierry Weber. Cambridge, Mass.: MIT Press, 1967.

Anders, Gunther. *Franz Kafka*, translated by A. Steer and A. K. Thorlby. New York: Hillary House, 1960.

Angress, R. K. "Kafka and Sacher-Masoch: A Note on *The Metamorphosis*." *MLN* 85 (1970): 745–46.

Angus, Douglas. "Kafka's *Metamorphosis* and 'The Beauty and the Beast' Tale." *JEGP* 52 (1954): 69–71.

Berkoff, Steven. The Trial *and* The Metamorphosis: *Two Theatre Adaptations from Franz Kafka*. Derbyshire, Eng.: Amber Lane Press, 1981.

Bernheimer, Charles. *Flaubert and Kafka: Studies in Psychopoetic Structure*, 186–87. New Haven: Yale University Press, 1982.

Binion, Rudolf. "What *The Metamorphosis* Means." *Symposium* 15 (1961): 214–20.

Blanchot, Maurice. "The Diaries: The Exigency of the Work of Art." Translated by Lyall H. Powers. In *Franz Kafka Today*, edited by Angel Flores and Homer Swander. Madison: University of Wisconsin Press, 1964.

Brown, Russell E. "A Mistake in *Die Verwandlung* of Kafka." *Germanic Notes* 16, no. 2 (1985): 19–21.

Camus, Albert. *The Myth of Sisyphus*, 126–27. New York: Knopf, 1955.

Cantrell, Carol Helmstetter. "*The Metamorphosis*: Kafka's Study of a Family." *Modern Fiction Studies* 23 (1978): 578–86.

Corngold, Stanley. *The Commentator's Despair: The Interpretation of Kafka's* Metamorphosis. Port Washington, N.Y.: Kennikat, 1973.

———. Introduction to his critical edition of *The Metamorphosis*. 11–22. New York: Bantam, 1972.

D'Haen, Theo. "The Liberation of the Samsas." *Neophilologus* 62, no. 2 (1978): 262–78.

Fickert, Kurt J. *Kafka's Doubles*, 47–49. Las Vegas: Lang, 1979.

Flores, Angel. *A Kafka Bibliography, 1908–1976*, 171–75. New York: Gordian Press, 1976.

———, ed. *The Kafka Problem*. New York: Octagon, 1963.

Fraiberg, Selma. "Kafka and the Dream." In *Modern Literary Criticism*, edited by Irving Howe. Boston: Beacon Press, 1958.

Friedman, Norman. "Kafka's *Metamorphosis*: A Literal Reading." *Approach* 49 (1963): 26–34.

————. "The Struggle of Vermin: Parasitism and Family Love in Kafka's *Metamorphosis*." *Forum* 9, no. 1 (1968): 23–32.

Gilman, Sander L. "A View of Kafka's Treatment of Actuality in *Die Verwandlung*." *Germanic Notes* 2, no. 4 (1971): 26–30.

Goldstein, Bluma. "Bachelors and Work: Social and Economic Conditions in "The Judgment," *The Metamorphosis*, and *The Trial*. In *The Kafka Debate*, edited by Angel Flores, 147–175. New York: Gordian Press, 1977.

Goodman, Paul. Preface to *The Metamorphosis by Franz Kafka*. New York: Vanguard, 1946.

Holland, Norman N. "Realism and Unrealism: Kafka's *Metamorphosis*." *Modern Fiction Studies* 4 (1958): 143–50.

Honig, Edwin. *Dark Conceit*, 63–68. New York: Oxford University Press, 1966.

Hoover, M. L. Introduction to her *Die Verwandlung*. London: Methuen, 1962.

Kuna, Franz. *Literature as Corrective Punishment*, 49–63. Bloomington: Indiana University Press, 1974.

Luke, F. D. "*The Metamorphosis*." In *Explain to Me Some Stories of Kafka*, edited by Angel Flores, 103–22. New York: Gordian Press, 1983.

MacAndrew, M. Elizabeth. "A Splacknuck and a Dung Beetle: Realism and Probability in Swift and Kafka." *College English* 31 (1969): 376–91.

McGlathery, James M. "Desire's Persecutions in Kafka's 'The Judgment,' *The Metamorphosis* and 'A Country Doctor.'" *Perspectives on Contemporary Literature* 7 (1981): 54–63.

Madden, William A. "A Myth of Mediation: Kafka's *Metamorphosis*." *Thought* 26 (1951): 246–66.

Mann, Thomas G. "Kafka's *Die Verwandlung* and Its Natural Model: An Alternative Reading." *University of Dayton Review* 15, no. 3 (1982): 65–74.

Martin, Peter. "The Cockroach as an Identification, with Reference to Kafka's *Metamorphosis*." *American Imago* 26 (1959): 65–71.

Parry, Idris F. "Kafka and Gogol." *German Life and Letters* 6 (1953): 141–45.

Poggioli, Renato. "Kafka and Dostoyevski." In *The Kafka Problem*, edited by Angel Flores, 97–107. New York: New Directions, 1946.

Politzer, Heinz. *Franz Kafka: Parable and Paradox*, 65–82. Ithaca: Cornell University Press, 1962.

Ramras, Rauch Gila. "Gregor Samsa in *The Metamorphosis*." In *The Protagonist in Transition: Studies in Modern Fiction*, 156–210. Berne: Lang, 1982.

Robertson, Ritenie. *Kafka: Judaism, Politics and Literature*. Oxford: Clarendon, 1982.

Rolleston, James. *Kafka's Narrative Theater*, 52–68. University Park: Pennsylvania State University Press, 1974.

Sokel, Walter. *Franz Kafka*, 19–22. New York: Columbia University Press, 1956.

————. "Kafka's *Metamorphosis*: Rebellion and Punishment." *Monatshefte* 48 (1956): 203–14.

————. *The Writer in Extremis*. Stanford, Calif.: Stanford University Press, 1959.

Spilka, Mark. "Kafka's Sources for *The Metamorphosis*." *Comparative Literature* 11 (1959): 289–307.

Springer, Mary D. "*The Metamorphosis*." In *Forms of the Modern Novella*. Chicago: University of Chicago Press, 1976.

Szanto, George H. *Narrative Consciousness: Structure and Reception in the Fiction of Franz*

Kafka, Beckett and Robbe-Grillet, 15–68, 173–80. Austin: University of Texas Press, 1972.

Tauber, Herbert. *Franz Kafka: An Interpretation of His Works*, 18–26. New Haven: Yale University Press, 1948.

Taylor, Alexander. "The Waking: The Theme of Kafka's *Metamorphosis*." *Studies in Short Fiction* 2 (1965): 337–42.

Thorlby, Anthony. *Kafka: A Study*, 34–40. London: Heinemann, 1972.

Tiefenbrun, Ruth. *Moment of Torment: An Interpretation of Franz Kafka's Short Stories*, 111–35. Carbondale: Southern Illinois University Press, 1973.

Urzidil, Johannes. *There Goes Kafka*, 82–96. Detroit: Wayne State University Press, 1968.

Vietta, Silvio. "Franz Kafka, Expressionism and Reification." In *Passion and Rebellion: The Expressionist Heritage*, edited by Stephen Eric Bronner and Douglas Kellner, 201–16. South Hadley, Mass.: Bergin, 1983.

Waldeck, Peter B. "Kafka's *Die Verwandlung* and 'Ein Hungerhunsther' as influenced by Leopold von Sacher-Masoch." *Monatshefte* 64 (1972): 147–52.

Webster, Peter Dow. "Franz Kafka's *Metamorphosis* as Death and Resurrection Fantasy." *American Imago* 16 (1959): 349–65.

Winkelman, John. "The Liberation of Gregor Samsa." In *Crisis and Commitment: Studies in German and Russian Literature*, edited by John Whiton and Harry Loewen, 237–46. Waterloo, Ontario: University of Waterloo Press, 1983.

Witt, Mary Ann. "Confinement in *Die Verwandlung* and *Les Sequestres d'Altona*." *Comparative Literature* 23 (1971): 32–44.

Wokenfeld, Suzanne. "Christian Symbolism in Kafka's *The Metamorphosis*." *Studies in Short Fiction* 10 (1973): 205–7.

Acknowledgments

"Gregor Samsa and Modern Spirituality" by Martin Greenberg from *The Terror of Art: Kafka and Modern Literature* by Martin Greenberg, © 1965, 1966, 1968 by Martin Greenberg. Reprinted by permission of Basic Books, Inc.

"Metamorphosis of the Metaphor" (originally entitled "Kafka's *Die Verwandlung*: Metamorphosis of the Metaphor") by Stanley Corngold from *Mosaic* 3, no. 4 (1970), "New Views on Franz Kafka," © 1970 by the University of Manitoba Press. Reprinted by permission.

"The Dramatic in Kafka's *Metamorphosis*" (originally entitled "The Dramatic in Kafka's Work to 1914") by Evelyn Torton Beck from *Kafka and the Yiddish Theatre: Its Impact on His Work* by Evelyn Torton Beck, © 1971 by the Regents of the University of Wisconsin. Reprinted by permission of the University of Wisconsin Press.

"*The Metamorphosis*" by Ronald Gray from *Franz Kafka* by Ronald Gray, © 1973 by Cambridge University Press. Reprinted by permission of Cambridge University Press.

"*Die Verwandlung*, Freud, and the Chains of Odysseus" by David Eggenschwiler from *Modern Language Quarterly* 39, no. 4 (December 1978), © 1979 by the University of Washington. Reprinted by permission.

"The Impersonal Narrator of *The Metamorphosis*" (originally entitled "The Impersonal Narrator of the Early Tales: *The Metamorphosis* [*Die Verwandlung*]") by Roy Pascal from *Kafka's Narrators: A Study of His Stories and Sketches* by Roy Pascal, © 1982 by Cambridge University Press. Reprinted by permission of Cambridge University Press.

"From Marx to Myth: The Structure and Function of Self-Alienation in Kafka's *Metamorphosis*" by Walter H. Sokel from *The Literary Review* 26, no. 4 (Summer 1983), © 1983 by Fairleigh Dickinson University. Reprinted by permission of the author.

"Kafka and Sacher-Masoch" by Mark M. Anderson from *The Kafka Society of America* 7, no. 2 (December 1983), © 1983 by the Kafka Society of America, Temple University. Reprinted by permission.

Index

Shakespeare, William, *Macbeth*, 11
"Silence of the Sirens, The" (Kafka),
  87–88
Sokel, Walter: on Kafka, 39, 43; on
  The Metamorphosis, 39–40, 50
Sparks, Kimberly, on *The Metamor-
  phosis*, 78
Strauss, Leo, 5

Talmud, Kafka on, 7
Three Essays on the Theory of Sexuality
  (Freud), 78–79
Tolstoy, Leo: influence of, on Kafka,
  30; *The Death of Ivan Ilyich*, 20, 30
Tonio Kroger (Mann), 66–67
Trial, The (Kafka), 31, 100
Trilling, Lionel: on Dostoevsky, 34; on
  Kafka, 34

"Urteil, Das." *See* "The Judgment"
Urzidil, Johannes, on Kafka, 39–40

Van den Berg, J. H., on Freud, 7
Venus in Furs (Sacher-Masoch), influence
  of, on *The Metamorphosis*, 120–21,
  124–25, 126–29, 130, 131, 133
Verwandlung, Die. See The Metamorphosis

"Wedding Preparations in the Country"
  (Kafka), 44–45, 73–74
Whitehead, Alfred North, *Science and
  the Modern World*, 34, 35
Wilson, Edmund, on Kafka, 31
Woolf, Virginia, and narration, 101
Writing, Kafka on, 48–49

Yahweh, nature of, 11

Zionism: and Kabbalah, 3–4, 12; Kafka
  and, 3–4, 12
Zvi, Sabbatai, 4, 13